W9-CBI-986

Additional Praise for *ONE PHONE CALL AWAY:*

"Only someone who has the knowledge and experience equal to that of Jeffrey Meshel deserves the right to tell the story with such authority. **Bravo to Jeff, the master networker!**"

> —Gorge A. Naddaff, Founder, Boston Market; Chairman and Co-CEO, KnowFat! Franchise Company

"Jeff Meshel is one of those **rare individuals who say what they believe** and does what he says. He has spent most of his adult life being helpful to others and in return his life is full of richness."

> —Richard Lavin, Cofounder, TIGER 21

"*One Phone Call Away* is an excellent guide on how to network effectively. Networking was a substantial factor in the success of every business I have been in and can make the difference between a business that does well and one that does not. I met Jeff at a dinner party a few years ago and, a few months later, closed a multimillion-dollar deal through an introduction he made. **The bottom line: Jeff's tips work!**"

> —Bob Diener, Cofounder, Hotels.com

"A must read! Jeff is the consummate networker! Amazing insights and steps to improve your own skills for a lifetime. If one follows his advice, it will definitely move you to the next level. The best investment you can make is to purchase this book!"

> —Larry Bartimer, hedge fund industry specialist

"Networking is one of the most essential tools in business. Yet few of us are ever taught how. Jeff Meshel is in **a league all his own when it comes to the art of building contacts.** He reveals his techniques and strategies with wit and wisdom. This must-read book is an invaluable tool for anyone wanting to get ahead in business and to take their network to the next level!"

—Susie Levan, Publisher, *Balance Magazine*

"As you well know, any one of us is just six telephone calls away from anyone in the world. Jeff is truly only one phone call away and this book will tell you why. More important, it will show you how to become a more effective networker, make more friends, and make more money. It's a great read and it will turn you into a one-person marketing machine! **I highly recommend it.**

—Shelly Palmer, Managing Director, Advanced Media Ventures Group, LLC; Vice President, National Academy of Television Arts & Sciences, New York

One Phone Call Away

One Phone Call Away

SECRETS OF A MASTER NETWORKER

JEFFREY W. MESHEL
with Douglas Garr

PORTFOLIO

I dedicate this book to
my beautiful children,
Benjamin and Talia

PORTFOLIO

Published by the Penguin Group

Penguin Group (USA) Inc., 375 Hudson Street, New York, New York 10014, U.S.A. • Penguin Group (Canada), 90 Eglinton Avenue East, Suite 700, Toronto, Ontario, Canada M4P 2Y3 (a division of Pearson Penguin Canada Inc.) • Penguin Books Ltd, 80 Strand, London WC2R 0RL, England • Penguin Ireland, 25 St. Stephen's Green, Dublin 2, Ireland (a division of Penguin Books Ltd) • Penguin Books Australia Ltd, 250 Camberwell Road, Camberwell, Victoria 3124, Australia (a division of Pearson Australia Group Pty Ltd • Penguin Books India Pvt Ltd, 11 Community Centre, Panchsheel Park, New Delhi – 110 017, India • Penguin Group (NZ), Cnr Airborne and Rosedale Roads, Albany, Auckland 1310, New Zealand (a division of Pearson New Zealand Ltd) • Penguin Books (South Africa) (Pty) Ltd, 24 Sturdee Avenue, Rosebank, Johannesburg 2196, South Africa

Penguin Books Ltd, Registered Offices:
80 Strand, London WC2R 0RL, England

First published in 2005 by Portfolio,
a member of Penguin Group (USA) Inc.

1   3   5   7   9   10   8   6   4   2

LIBRARY OF CONGRESS CATALOGING IN PUBLICATION DATA

Meshel, Jeff.
One phone call away : secrets of a master networker / Jeff Meshel ; with Doug Garr.
p.   cm.
Includes index.
ISBN 1-59184-090-2
1. Social networks.   2. Interpersonal relations.   I. Garr, Doug.   II. Title.
HM741.M47 2005
650.1'3—dc22   2005050954

Printed in the United States of America
Set in Life
Designed by Joy O'Meara

Acknowledgments

Every book has its own distinct genesis, and *One Phone Call Away* is no different. The book you are holding in your hands is a direct result of networking. Let me connect the dots:

After a few attempts to sell this book to a publisher, unsolicited, I discovered that an author can increase his odds considerably once he has a literary agent. For some time I had admired author Harvey Mackay, who has written several books about business, perhaps most notably *Swim with the Sharks*. It occurred to me that I knew Mackay's son-in-law, Larry Bartimer, and got in touch with him. He suggested that I call Mackay's agent directly. And so I met Jonathon Lazear, who immediately saw the possibilities of an early version of my manuscript. Lazear found publisher Adrian Zackheim (who coincidentally had been the publisher behind *Swim with the Sharks Without Being Eaten Alive*), who then teamed me up with author Doug Garr. Garr helped me find precise, clear, and concise language. Editor Megan Casey's editorial judgment was instrumental in shaping our prose.

I would like to thank all my colleagues at the Strategic Forum for their input and advice on networking over the past few years. When I mentioned the idea of writing such a book, they offered encouragement, advice, and support. This finished product would be a lot less without The Forum. Specifically, I owe a huge debt of gratitude to my guest contributors in chapter 10, John Oden, Jeff Bauman, and David Gensler. These three gentlemen are expert at what they do and bring their own philosophies to the networking banquet table. Sy Siegal convinced me that I had to include a chapter on people with shy personalities. I spent a lot of time bouncing ideas off the desk of my good friend Richard Lavin. I'm much obliged to him.

Finally, I'd like to thank my two children, Benjamin and Talia, who continue to provide the love, motivation, and support I need to achieve goals I might never have thought possible.

I also have a networking thank-you.

In considering all the elements of this book, an issue developed regarding the jacket. Portfolio liked one; I liked another. I was pretty adamant, so I suggested that we let my database of contacts decide. So I sent out both jackets—and received 1,300 responses. Those responses were the catalyst for open-minded discussions that led to the cover.

So I want to thank all those in my database who took the time to render an opinion.

Contents

Introduction

Everyone has heard the expression, "It's not what you know. It's who you know." It is probably one of our greatest business adages. But equally important, *it's what* you know *about* who you know. These aphorisms are the most revealing of truths.

Of course, what you know is vitally important, because in today's competitive world people want to deal primarily with smart professionals who are very good at what they do. But when there's such a big pool of talented people to choose from, there must be another level of distinction.

What, then, differentiates you from the rest of the group? Stop here and think for a moment. You're an accountant, you're a lawyer, you're a salesman, you're a manager in a large corporation, or you're running a small business. You're in a fungible world. So how can you stand out from the pack? What makes you different or, better yet, special? If you don't have an answer, or you're searching for an answer, my intent is to help you find it. Or create it.

At the end of the day, you want as many connectors as possible. Referrals come from friends, relatives, or colleagues who know someone you don't—and can connect you to him or her.

In John Guare's well-known play, *Six Degrees of Separation*, everyone is only six times removed in circumstance or acquaintance from every other person on the planet. Mind blowing? Absolutely. Especially once you get a handle on how it works.

I believe that your next sale, your next deal, your *ultimate success,* is just one phone call away—or one degree of separation. The power of who you know, and what you know about who you know, is immeasurable and creates huge opportunities. Networking is a recognizable, quantifiable thing.

I'd like to make one thing clear right away. It's my feeling that networking has been a victim of bad public relations. Somehow, networking has been equated with hustling or overt solicitation. In the past, there was nothing subtle about a networker. His methodology began with the cocktail party pronouncement: "Excuse me, I've got to work the room." A person who is "selling" was often considered by more reserved people as somewhat vulgar and in some echelons as a user, a freeloader, or an unsavory person.

Be certain of this: There's nothing negative about being a good networker. To some degree, I believe it's a hackneyed term. There is a difference between arrogance and confidence, but it's a subtle one and straddles a very fine line. Being bold and straightforward doesn't have to be equated with being smug and conceited. You can sound knowledgeable without being pompous. You can forge valuable business bonds without feeling like you're constantly trying to "use" somebody. Part of this attitude comes from modulating your mind-set.

On its deepest level, networking isn't about using people. It's about giving something of yourself. Contrary to the thinking of "what's in it for me?"

Many people in the business world believe that networking is simply intrinsic to a certain type of personality. You're either good at it or not so good at it, and that's all there is to it. I've got good news: Networking isn't genetic. Just because it wasn't ordained at birth, it doesn't mean you can't acquire it.

———

You may be skeptical. I understand that and anticipated it before writing this book. But every day the world of commerce expands and becomes more relationship based. Every day, someone in power makes an important hiring or buying decision based on the simple fact that he or she "knows" the person, or knows someone else who can attest to a person's ability and character, and not just that the person in question can do the job.

If you're the type of person who sits on his hands and waits for business to walk through your door, you're making a huge mistake. When business is good, you probably never have to pick up the phone. When it's pouring outside, you likely don't think about rainmaking.

It's not enough to say, "I guess I better get up from behind my desk and pound the pavement a bit." If you don't develop an extensive list of clients and potential customers, you may be headed for an unexpected slump, or worse. If you don't take a more serious look at networking, you're not only missing deals and sales that you're not even aware of but you may also be putting your business or career in serious jeopardy.

I don't mean to sound intimidating. The ideas in this book are simple, simple, simple! There's no special alchemy involved. Perhaps, surprisingly, they are rooted in common sense and simple techniques that anyone can learn to apply.

Networking is arguably an art or a science, or perhaps even a combination of both. But it is not a difficult science, nor is it an opaque art. It is not without form or structure. Understand a vital point: Networking is not a theory. It is an actual practice. It's not specifically taught at Harvard Business School (though getting a degree from a place like that certainly opens doors—something that every applicant and graduate already knows and relies on). Perhaps it should be, so we can remove any trace of denigration from its meaning. (There are still some private clubs that forbid members from taking out note pads in the dining room. How presumptuous to think the members actually may be doing business over lunch!)

Some people are naturals, people born to network. But it's my contention that it is simply an acquired skill, just like any other. You can become an excellent networker if you are disciplined, open minded, willing to share, and willing to make the necessary effort to learn how to do it.

Most business people don't realize the value of their acquaintances and the relationships they have. There are more than five thousand people in my personal database. Obviously, I don't know all of them well, but I have enough information about most of the people so that at some point I could call on them. More important, if any one of them calls on me, I am in a position to recall the necessary data and help them. Every day I add new friends and acquaintances; in the past two decades I have become the go-to guy for many of my relationships. My colleagues often tell me that they've passed on a referral by saying, "Call Jeff Meshel; he knows everyone." It's a flattering comment. You can be that kind of person. I want you to be conscious of who you know, and I want you to maximize the benefit of every relationship. Networking is much more than meeting someone and exchanging business cards. As you'll read, it's what you do *after* you make the initial contact that matters.

Most people need help understanding how to network. Becoming sensitive to the needs of others is paramount for success. Networking is a discipline that can and should start before one even begins a business career. The first hurdle in networking is to realize that it is one of the most vital skills you can have in your repertoire—that it's something learnable, and stands you in better stead for success. It's just a tool but an extremely valuable one.

In the course of this book I will return to three major themes: the power of developing relationships, how to sell yourself, and how to always do the right thing. I believe each of these themes to be essential to increasing your networking abilities and business capabilities, which are so reliant upon each other as to be indiscernible.

I recently had lunch with a very dear friend, Peter, who is a stockbroker at one of the large New York City firms and like all private-wealth guys wants to build his client base. He isn't doing badly, but it isn't like the glory days of pre-Internet meltdown. He is fortunate in that he is very personable and has the appropriate skills to really excel. Yet he is not a guy who immediately warms to the expression "it's who you know," though he's in precisely the business where it matters most.

I tried to convince him about the power of networking and getting involved in additional platforms. I explained how every contact he has is a potential resource. I told him to try to help people and good things will happen in return. He picked uncomfortably at his Caesar salad. He wanted to agree with me, but he couldn't. *He doesn't get it.*

I continued to prod him. I discovered that Peter plays recreational softball. He lives in a very affluent neighborhood. I asked him if he knows what his teammates do for a living. He proudly answered, "No, I don't want to mix sports with business. All of these guys are there to play ball. It's an escape from the daily grind. The last thing they want to talk about is their work."

I sensed that he feared that he was crossing the line and might be perceived improperly. I tried to explain that he doesn't have to sell his services. If he knew what his teammates did for a living, he could potentially make referrals and help his teammates. Do things for others and these good deeds will come back. His response was that he feels funny about being "pushy." It is not about hard selling, or even soft selling. It's not about asking people directly for favors. It's not about doing business in the on-deck circle. It's about building relationships and trust. It's about making yourself approachable.

By dessert, I had become somewhat agitated about not getting through to him. "Peter, if you asked one of your teammates what they do and then said, 'I know someone who may be synergistic to your business,' do you think he wouldn't be interested? You're not selling to him. You are trying to help him.

"I have never met anyone who doesn't want to meet someone else who could be a good business contact. Your teammates will appreciate your efforts, I promise. They may ultimately do business with you or refer someone to you because you went out of your way for them."

Peter's story can be prophetic in a negative way, if you allow it to be. If you don't ask, you don't receive.

Have you ever had a friend suggest to you that you weren't exploring enough potential business opportunities through friends, relatives, and people you just met? Were you somewhat reserved when you heard this kind of criticism? Or did you nod your head in agreement and then fail to act in a positive way? Have you ever found yourself reacting to advice the way my friend Peter did?

If you've answered yes to any of these questions, then you're putting yourself at a serious disadvantage in your career and business. The next time you're at a business function try to categorize the various guests whom you don't know at all. Is there a person in a group who is controlling a conversation where three or four others are hanging on their every word? Is there a person off in a corner, nursing a glass of wine without attempting to meet anyone? Which person would you rather be?

I admit that Peter had me frustrated. He listened, he understood, but he won't act. At the end of the day, we all have to help ourselves. I don't expect you to do everything I do, but I know you will relate to some of my experiences and beliefs. If you follow some of my suggestions I guarantee you great results.

The world continually faces very challenging times. Recently, oil has been as high as $65 a barrel. U.S. currency, valued against the euro, is hitting all-time lows. Alan Greenspan, in describing Fed policies, said, "There are bubbles all over, and we are going to deal with them." Though the nation's vital signs are fairly positive, there is a considerable amount of coughing and sputtering, despite a stock market rally in 2005. The economy is taking one step forward, one step backward. Analysts and economists are sometimes bitterly divided on whether U.S. business results are sporadic and fleeting or really indicate a long-term move forward. Interest rates are near fifty-year lows but are slowly moving north. Major companies have filed for bankruptcy protection, white-collar criminals are still in the news almost daily, pension funds are substantially underfunded, and foreclosures are at all-time highs. There is still a certain amount of nervousness in the air surrounding any good economic news. And all bets are off if there's another cataclysmic event due to terrorist activity.

Let's say, for example, you're a small business owner and you've just discovered the potential to sell your products internationally. Perhaps you already have a few contacts in Europe. But what about China? The largest nation on earth is now wide open for commerce, and many business analysts expect it to be a major U.S. trading partner in the coming years. There may be great opportunities there. You'd like to pick up the phone and make a call, but I'll bet you don't know a single soul in Beijing.

What can you do to create more opportunities for yourself? My answer is to expand the list of *who* you know.

●   ●   ●

I'd like you to take the following test:

Take a quick scan of the following list of names. Maybe you can circle familiar names as you go. You'll see they are common surnames. Some you will recognize, others you won't.

Algazi, Alvarez, Alpern, Ametrano, Andrews, Aran, Arnstein, Ashford, Bailey, Ballout, Bamberger, Baptista, Barr, Barrows, Baskerville, Bassiri, Bell, Bokgese, Brandao, Bravo, Brooke, Brightman, Billy, Blau, Bohen, Bohn, Borsuk, Brendle, Butler, Calle, Cantwell, Carrell, Chinlund, Cirker, Cohen, Collas, Couch, Callegher, Calcaterra, Cook, Crowley, Curbelo, Dellamana, Diaz, Dirar, Duncan, D'Agostino, Delakas, Dillon, Donaghey, Daly, Dawson, Edery, Ellis, Elliott, Eastman, Easton, Famous, Fermin, Fialco, Finklestein, Farber, Falkin, Feinman, Friedman, Gardner, Gelpi, Glascock, Grandfield, Greenbaum, Greenwood, Gruber, Garil, Goff, Gladwell, Greenup, Gannon, Granshaw, Garcia, Gennis, Gerard, Gericke, Gilbert, Glassman, Glazer, Gomendio, Gonzalez, Greenstein, Guglielmo, Gurman, Haberkorn, Hoskins, Hussein, Hamm, Hardwick, Harrell, Hauptman, Hawkins, Henderson, Hayman, Hibara, Hehmann, Herbst, Hedges, Hogan, Hoffman, Horowitz, Hsu, Huber, Ikiz, Jaroschy, Johann, Jacobs, Jara, Johnson, Kassel, Keegan, Kuroda, Kavanau, Keller, Kevill, Kiew, Kimbrough, Ramos, Regan, Reisman, Renkert, Roberts, Rowan, Rene, Rosario, Rothbart, Saperstein, Schoenbrod, Schwed, Sears, Statosky, Stutphen, Sheehy, Silverton, Silverman, Silverstein, Sklar, Slotkin, Speros, Stollman, Sadowski, Schles, Shapiro, Sigdel, Snow, Spencer, Steinkol, Stewart, Stires, Stopnik, Stonehill, Tayss, Tilney, Temple, Torfield, Townsend, Trimpin, Turchin, Villa, Vasillov, Voda, Waring, Weber, Weinstein, Wang, Wegimont, Weed, Weishaus.

This list of 250 surnames was taken from the Manhattan phone book. Now, identify the names of people you know with the same last names. Now, add up who you know, your "networking quotient." For example, if you know three people whose last name is Cohen, you get three points; two people whose last name is Wang, you get two points; and so on. For every additional name you know you get one point.

According to Malcolm Gladwell, author of *The Tipping Point*, people with a special gift for bringing people together are "connectors." Connectors tend to know a lot of people. Gladwell gave a similar test to about four hundred people. The results varied. A group of students in their late teens or early twenties knew about twenty-one people on the average. A group of health educators and academics in their forties and fifties, largely white, highly educated, and wealthy, had an average score of thirty-nine.

The difference in the scores wasn't surprising. College students don't have as wide a circle of contacts as people in their forties. In every group tested, there was a wide range between the highest and the lowest scorers. In Gladwell's sample, the low score was nine and the high score was 118.

What is your score? If you are unpleasantly surprised, you probably should make a greater effort to expand who you know.

I am a connector, but it also means I am a collector. Every person I meet goes into my database. My sensors are always tuned in to whatever environment I'm in. I thrive on putting people together. When something good happens from an introduction, it makes my day. I create a lot of opportunities—both business and social—for a great number of people, and at the end of the day so many good things come back to me.

My philosophy isn't for everyone. It isn't a quick fix, where after six weeks you're transformed from a totally introverted person into an outgoing, accomplished networker. If you think only about yourself, the likelihood that people will think of you is greatly diminished. Most people are *me* oriented and won't immediately think they can be a good networker. If you're too egocentric, too self-centered, and cannot fathom the notion of trying to change some of your daily habits, none of my recommendations will take hold.

I have given a lot of thought about how to convey to others what I know about networking. I am living proof of the power you can gain by building and nurturing new relationships. I am only one phone call away from reaching someone I need. I realized that it isn't a matter of following perfunctory rules. A great networker has to be outgoing and a giver. The best are good salesmen, too. Selling a product or a service or yourself all have common traits and skills. I discuss "selling" in a general way at the beginning of this book. It relates directly to improving your ability to meet new business contacts, form networks, and increase the results in your chosen career.

It is my hope that the following pages will make you more knowledgeable and more effective. *I hope to show you how networking can enrich your career, your business, and your everyday relationships. After reading this book, I want you to be conscious of who you know and how to maximize the potential of every new person you meet.*

Part One

THE
BASICS

1

Twenty-one and Green
What I Learned from My Past

I am sure you have heard the expression, "I would rather be lucky than smart." There are many unlucky smart people who can't make a living. Then there are those very lucky individuals who don't know what day of the week it is yet still earn spectacular incomes. How about those lucky people who were born into the right family? This has to be the greatest degree of good luck. How many people do you know that either live off an inheritance or go into the family business?

Then there are the rest of us who venture into the world of commerce and stake our own claim. We are without question the vast majority.

> **Rule 1**
> What you know facilitates who you know. What you know dictates how lucky you become.

I'm forty-eight and president of a company called Mercury Capital, which I started and built with my partner. We specialize in bridge loans, primarily offering short-term financing to businesses and individuals who use real property as collateral. I often reflect on what I know and think how fortunate I would have been if I had the knowledge contained within these pages when I was starting out. Today, I try to be a sponge by reading everything relevant to my interests. I always feel the need to know more. I plow through four newspapers every morning, not just for business but to stay informed on the events of the world. Your prime currency is always knowing what's going on around you. Your colleagues, your clients, your friends—even your competitors—will respect you more if you're well informed.

When I graduated from New York University in 1980, I was a typical twenty-one-year-old. I really had no idea what I wanted to do with my life. As an accounting and finance major, my short-term plan (the word "goal" might be too much of a stretch) was modest and typical—to get a job at one of the Big Eight firms with a starting salary of $17,000 per year. But the thought of spending twenty or thirty years working for one of these shops was very unappealing and daunting. The climb to partner meant conforming to a standard corporate behavior model. I didn't fit that mold. I was a young man in a hurry. Also, I wasn't sure I wanted to spend my life being a numbers cruncher.

I had entrepreneurial genes in my bloodlines. My dad had owned a couple of gas stations. Every day he rose at 5:00 A.M. and came home at 7:00 P.M. swathed in grease. Today's news stories about $3.00 a gallon for gas? That's not a crisis. At least we can buy it. During the 1970s, there were gas lines around the block with cars waiting to fill up. Back then, the media compared the situation with gas rationing in World War II. The last number on your license plate—odd or even—dictated which day of the week you could buy gas. People were very appreciative that they could get gas at all. That's a crisis.

I saw the oil shortage during my high school years as an opportunity to learn the valuable experience of interacting in a retail service business. Not only did I make good tips but also it helped shape my business character at an early age. Today, I frequently urge high school kids to get retail jobs to learn how to interact comfortably with consumers in a business environment. The experience is invaluable and essential. Nearly every executive who has had retail experience will tell you how important it was. The seemingly routine sales job enhanced their perception, communication, and understanding of their customers. It inculcated confidence, which increased comfort.

The year after I earned my degree, the job market wasn't great. The opportunities seemed sparse. About the only thing I had going for me was that I thought I knew what I *didn't* want to do.

When I told my dad that I didn't want to work for him, he was disappointed, to say the least. I respected his success and his work ethic, but I just didn't have the same passion for cars. I didn't care about what went on under the hood. It rankled him that his dream of Meshel and Son did not work out. But I had a college degree, and he didn't, and that was a major difference.

So, there I was only twenty-one, grappling with the infamous question: What am I going to do with my life? Like most of my friends, I had no idea. It finally occurred to me that some of my parents' friends were very successful, owned their own businesses, and probably would have some valuable insights on the job front. I compiled a list and asked my mother if I could call them to ask them their opinions.

The first person I made an appointment with was a man by the name of Mr. Cantor, who owned Empire Sporting Goods, a very successful company in lower Manhattan that sold T-shirts and other apparel. He and my father had been friends since they were children. Cantor's secretary was very gracious and immediately booked an appointment for me.

I remember the meeting as if it were yesterday. When I arrived at Cantor's office, I was asked to wait in the reception area.

I wasn't really very nervous—anxious was more like it. After fidgeting for half an hour, I began to feel very insignificant. Why was I kept waiting so long? Was this standard behavior in the business world? Perhaps Cantor's manners weren't very refined. Perhaps I had to learn patience.

Finally, a secretary announced, "Mr. Meshel, Mr. Cantor will see you now."

I'll never forget the scene I walked into. Mr. Cantor was on the phone, and he didn't seem to be in any hurry to finish the call. I sat directly in front of him while he continued his conversation. He didn't acknowledge my presence, and at one point he turned his chair around and I stared at his back until he eventually hung up. It was demeaning. I never felt so small.

"Jeff, it's so nice to see you," he finally said. "I understand you want to speak to me. I know you just graduated and are probably looking for a job. Unfortunately, right now business is a little slow and we are not bringing on any new people."

I thought to myself, *"Wow, he doesn't waste any time."*

"Mr. Cantor, I didn't come to ask you for a job."

"Oh, so what can I do for you?"

"Well, I've known of you and your business for many years. It's obvious that you have built a highly recognized brand and your products are being sold in all of the sporting goods stores in New York. I'm sure that creating a success like you have didn't come easy and you learned a lot in the process."

"That's for sure."

"Well, you obviously have a lot more experience than I do and have achieved heights that I only hope for. I also know that there had to be bumps in the road, wrong decisions, and moments where you said to yourself, 'If only I did this differently.'

"You're a knowledgeable, seasoned businessman, which brings me to ask, if you were twenty-one again and knew what you know now, what would you do differently? What business career would you pursue?"

Perhaps I didn't understand exactly what I was doing, but in hindsight, I realized that I was already learning how to sell myself, in a very subtle way. I was performing an exercise in flattery and orchestration. I simply placed Mr. Cantor on a pedestal. My goal was to make him feel as if I was in complete awe of him. Not exactly easy, given the rude introduction I'd just received a few moments ago.

Mr. Cantor didn't reply right away. He picked up his phone, buzzed his secretary, and told her to hold his calls. He gathered his thoughts and spoke for the next hour or so about what he did, what he should have done, the mistakes he made, and what he would do if he were my age now.

I sat there listening intently, absorbing his advice.

"If I were twenty-one today I would go to Wall Street," he began, and then explained all the opportunities that existed in the investment world.

I placed Mr. Cantor in the rarefied air of achievement and gave him the opportunity to instruct me.

This was a big event in my life at the time. I went from being looked on as a nuisance, perhaps, to someone Mr. Cantor opened his mind to. He conveyed his insights and wisdom, and I learned the value of absorbing all the free advice I could get. I was able to change the way he viewed me. And from that, I also learned the value of controlling a situation.

> **Rule 2**
>
> Make the person you are speaking with feel like he or she is the most important person you know (relatively speaking, of course).

Today, I receive frequent calls from clients and friends asking me if I will advise their son or daughter. My wife's niece, Lisa Klein, who lives in Florida, asked me for similar advice when she was younger. I advised her to go to work in my friend's restaurant as a waitress. My logic was that for a short period of time it would be a good experience. She'll learn to talk to people; she'll experience rude people; she'll experience polite people; she'll know how to get someone who may be on edge to be a little more relaxed. Her mother was dead set against it. "It's demeaning," she told me. I disagreed. "It's not demeaning. It's anything but demeaning. It will be a tremendous life lesson. She'll learn what it's like to interact with all kinds of people."

Lisa took the job and loved it. She became much more comfortable talking to people. She saw some people were gracious and others who weren't and looked down at her. She learned how to immediately get your perception of self to change. ("Perception of self" is different from "self-perception." Self-perception is how I perceive myself. Perception of self is how I perceive the person perceiving me.) I'd say to always be extra polite and inquisitive, know her product, which is the food the chef is preparing—and know what's really good. Then she could say, "By the way, I happen to know this dish is excellent. Or, if you like seafood, I would recommend the mahi mahi, it's fresh every day. I've had it myself."

Going out of your way for people is like planting a field with seeds. The more seeds you plant the more likely a tree will grow. In my business career I have harvested quite a few trees. And they sprout up in the least likely places at times that are impossible to predict. You never know where they might land. I already have received business that came to me from an appreciative twenty-one-year-old who now is twenty-seven and very successful at Goldman Sachs. I wound up doing a bridge loan, thanks to one of his referrals, and my firm earned a couple of hundred thousand dollars.

One of my main objectives is to be just one phone call away from getting to any resource that I might need.

Everyone's first real job is a momentous event.

> **Rule 3**   At each new stage of life we don't "graduate from," we "graduate to."

Do you remember how nervous you were? It is probably one of the most awkward times of your life, certainly of your career. Usually, you begin at the lowest level on the corporate food chain. You have little or no credibility. You even have to grovel to the mail-room staff. Or you are the mail-room staff. You have to earn your colleagues' respect. You're just a rookie.

Worst of all, you don't know anybody. If you are selling a product or service, you are probably cold-calling people with the hope of getting a shot at converting them into buying something you're selling. The experience is unsettling and fraught with rejection. However, when the first piece of business comes your way, the gratification is exhilarating. It's the foundation to building a clientele.

SOME HOT RESULTS FROM COLD CALLS

Before the stock market's 2000 collapse, I received at least a call a week from cold callers pitching me a stock that few people knew about and "couldn't miss." For the last few years, the number of calls waned considerably. Now that the market has recovered (although not yet to the level of the turn-of-the-millennium peak), the calls have begun again. The callers are obviously tutored on an effective approach (a pitch sheet), and they are almost always overly aggressive. Most of them are unknowledgeable, and simply come at me head on without thinking about me. A few, however, are exceptionally good. (I always listen to their pitches and am polite with them even though I would never consider doing business with any of them.)

You might recall the 2000 movie *Boiler Room* where young, unsophisticated hustlers are hired by an unscrupulous stock brokerage firm to cold-call unsuspecting investors to buy stocks that the firm is promoting. In this film the brokerage firm is a bogus operation and their stock investments are scams. Their approach was a classic "pump and dump" scheme. But a lot of their techniques are used by legitimate businesses. It would surprise you as to how many brokers have built their businesses by cold calling.

Now think about being on the other end. I don't think there's a single person in America who hasn't been called at least once by a telemarketer. Those who have had the unenviable experience of being accosted several times—often during dinner, no doubt—probably know the difference between the occasional good seller and the all-too-common bad ones. Most of us are conditioned to say no thanks and hang up before the pitchman can get his hooks into you. Why? Because they are impersonal and follow a standard-issue crib sheet where they begin by blandly saying, "How are you today, Mr. Meshel?" We sense immediately that this approach is anything but sincere. The caller doesn't care a whit how you feel; he's simply asking the least offensive question to keep you on the line. They're trained to read the script in a breathless monotone, hoping you won't slam the receiver down until they're finished. It might as well be an automated call with a recorded voice (which, pathetically, some already are).

But think for a moment how you might respond if a caller began, "Hello, Mr. Meshel. Forgive me for calling you at home, but I got your name from a list of people who might be interested in certain products and services my firm is offering. I'd like to explain them if this is a good time to talk. If not, I'd be happy to try you at some more convenient hour." This softer approach does several things: It casts the caller as warm and understanding, and it shows respect for the person's time. It attempts to break down the natural defenses people have toward intrusive, unsolicited pitches. And it expresses a level of candor you don't normally hear.

I have firsthand experience as a cold caller. Early in my career I was working for a real estate syndicator, and my job was to sell tax-sheltered real estate investments. Every morning I would go to work and pull out lists of accountants provided by the American Institute of Certified Public Accountants. I focused on the South and just kept calling, hoping to solicit interest. Miraculously, I hit a hot streak in Asheville, North Carolina, of all places. There I found a little regional firm where the managing partner loved these types of real estate transactions. He became a long-term client and friend, and he helped me to raise millions of dollars.

I discovered one useful fact from cold calling. It doesn't work well in New York, where people are in a hurry and lead frenzied lives. They're inundated with pitches from everywhere, have their guard up all the time, and it's next to impossible to penetrate it. New Yorkers are just not receptive. But cold calling seems to be effective in parts of the country where the typical lifestyle is less frenetic and people are more approachable.

For the most part, however, cold calling is a frustrating experience. You need to be motivated, disciplined, sincere, a skillful conversationalist, and well informed to be successful.

So how do you get the person on the other end of the line to hang on instead of hang up? That's actually a phenomenal challenge for those of us that enjoy being challenged.

It helps to be highly organized. I used the following device, a contact sheet. Here is a partial listing of the results.

DATE	NAME	CONVERSATION
6/22	J. Spirit	Spoke about investment; call next Wednesday.
6/22	B. Jones	Will show it to his CPA; follow up next week with a call.
6/22	L. Kahn	Call in two days set up appointment.
6/22	S. Fox	Will run by his CPA.
6/22	N. Karson	Call in two weeks.
6/22	L. Levine	Call next Wednesday to set up appointment.
6/22	N. Kas	Probably will do it; call his partner, Tom.
6/22	M. Donaghue	Long conversation; had him on the ropes.
6/22	P. Hallie	Not too bright; will talk to his financial advisor.
6/22	S. Lassiter	Invested in company products; stay on him.

My goal every day was to fill in a full sheet of actual conversations. I set my own productivity goal of forty calls per day. I know this sheet seems simple, but it really motivated me. At the end of the week I would review all the connections I made. Cold calling is a numbers game; the success rate is a pretty fixed (and, I might add, low) percentage. So the more calls you make, and the more organized you are about following up, the greater the result. If you are insecure, you probably will not be successful. If you do not know how to think quickly and respond to difficult questions, you will not do well. I'm not suggesting you consider telemarketing as a career. But the lessons you learn and the experience you get from spending days with a headset on are translatable to almost any business you pursue.

The following is a list of things you should do to prepare yourself before you make that first call in any business:

> ➤ Know your product and the competing products intimately. The first time a prospective customer asks you a question and you attempt to bluff with sketchy knowledge, you're finished.

> ➤ If you are asked a question that is technical in nature or is not within your scope of knowledge, have somebody available in your company who can respond to the question.

> ➤ Be prepared to discuss the advantages and disadvantages of your product and your competitor's. Good sales people who are skillful with the pluses and minuses will immediately earn a customer's respect.

> ➤ Be well informed about the economy and relevant news issues. Magazines, newspapers, and specific trade journals relative to your business should be required reading.

> ➤ Be ready for rejection and learn the difference between "I have no interest in your product [at all]," and "I have no interest at this time." The latter response means the door is still open.

> ➤ Keep accurate records of your contacts and keep a complete database continually updated. This will help you mine new fields and avoid wasting time covering old ground.

Rule 4

Good judgment comes from experience. Experience comes from bad judgment.

Why does one cold call work and another one doesn't? Why are you not capturing the attention of the audience that you're speaking to? If you keep getting rejected, what can you do to improve your results? How do you turn no into maybe, and maybe into yes? The answers to these questions revolve around developing proper sales techniques, like being able to read the person you're speaking to and reacting to the way they react to you.

The benefit of this type of learning experience is not quantitative, it's qualitative. Because it's so hard, few people like doing it. But then you'll ask someone who's successful, who started their career cold calling, and he or she'll tell you how powerful it was for them as an early learning experience. If you understand how cold calling relates to the way you approach any phase of any business, then you are on your way to mastering some of the ideas in this book.

2

Networking Fundamentals

Ben Hogan, one of golf's legends, was known for his classic swing, intense work ethic, and his quirky, guarded personality. Famously laconic, he avoided friendly banter on the course during competition. Once, when an interviewer asked what the secret to his game was, Hogan replied that the secret was "in the dirt." Since he never elaborated, golf pundits generally have construed his answer to mean endless practice. In short, what Hogan meant was there is no secret. Logical enough, I suppose. But I've always felt that story goes further. All great golfers—all athletes and all successful people, for that matter—have one thing in common. They master the fundamentals. They may not grip the clubs in exactly the same way or swing in precisely the same motion, but every teaching pro will tell you there are three or four basic components that never vary. They can dissect the videos and show you how every single successful golfer does certain *simple* things the same way.

The same philosophy applies to business. Understanding and implementing networking fundamentals are essential to building your resources and contacts. Some of these tenets will seem obvious. Yet I am often amazed at how many people I come across in business who forsake the basics. And, of course, like athletes, you must continue to work on these skills all the time. Complete mastery is the goal, and if you're humble, as skilled as you eventually become, you know that mastery is never really complete.

One of the most telling examples is a businessman who is a self-professed expert in networking. I'll call him David. In fact, he is currently writing a book about networking. David is highly regarded in venture capital circles, and his reputation has grown to a point where he speaks to industry groups all over the country. He is known for his ability to raise large sums of money; investors obviously have a great deal of trust in him. When I first met him, I had a brief but engaging conversation with him, and I thought it would be beneficial for us to meet at some point. You never know where there might be synergies between his firm and mine. Some of his clients are potential resources for areas of business I have interests in. He was very responsive. I ended by saying that he'd be sure to hear from me, and he said he'd look forward to my call.

The following week I phoned David to set up an appointment and left word that I called. He never called me back. This was odd—perhaps he didn't get the message. So I called again and left another message. Again, he never called back. Many people might not interpret this as unusual. You meet someone, it goes well, you both promise to follow up, and then when the time comes, the person you plan to have lunch with is now unconcerned with what transpired. It is no longer a priority; he is too busy, or some other reason. We are not supposed to take these slights personally, but I do. I was rankled by this behavior.

A couple of months later, I bumped into David again at a cocktail party. I went over and introduced myself again and told him that I called him three times, and that he never returned my call.

"Oh, Jeff, I'm sorry," he said. "I really am not good at returning phone calls. If you want to get hold of me the best way to communicate is by e-mail." Okay, I thought to myself. He is quirky, but I don't want to burn any bridges—every contact is important to me. It's still a ridiculous response. I happen to be a seasoned businessman, however, and I've trained myself always to overlook minor idiosyncrasies.

The following day I e-mailed David and suggested that we get together. Once again, I did not receive a response after several days. I was surprised that someone like David could be so remiss. Thereafter, I forgot about him until he was invited down to a meeting of an association of which I'm a member. (It's called the Strategic Forum, and I'll explain more about it in a later chapter.) David was the guest speaker. Ironically, his presentation topic was the fundamentals of networking. "*You can't be serious,*" I thought.

After his speech, I told him, "David, I'm puzzled. You just outlined all the fundamentals that you consider being paramount in order to be a good networker. You may recall that I tried to get together with you several times. First I called you, then, at your suggestion I e-mailed you, and you never returned my call or my e-mail. You seem to be rather negligent in the basics."

"Jeff, I'm sorry," he said. "I'm really just not good at getting back to people."

I was shocked. Is he so busy, or so unorganized, or so arrogant that he just assumes he's not offending people like me who he meets in his daily business travels?

I think David is an enigma. I'm not sure what you think. But I'm certain that his failure to respond in any capacity—even a "sorry, I just don't have the time right now"—damaged his credibility. I would never refer a client or a piece of business to him, and I'm certainly in the position to do so. I view him as one of those guys who has been lucky, and not particularly farsighted in his thinking, or even very smart.

Now, what if David had said to himself, "What's my downside if I have lunch with Jeff? Probably none. I'll invest two hours of my day, and who knows what will happen? Maybe we have a few contacts in common? I have nothing to lose." Had he decided to meet with me, I would have learned about his business and needs. He lost out because he didn't know that I have a particular avocation and like to make strategic introductions that open up doors for people. I could have been a great resource for his next big deal. But he will never know, will he?

Months later, I was having a conversation with a friend of mine who told me that he also had met David at an event and knew of his reputation as well. He had an engaging conversation with him and followed up. He also never got a return phone call or even a note thanking him for his offer to do him a favor in reference to a mutual business contact. My friend's impression was the same as mine. I probably would not be so harsh about David if he was a regular business contact, but he is supposed to be an authority on networking.

TRAINING DAYS

Here's a question I'd like you to consider: What do former President Clinton and the CEO of IBM have in common? The obvious answer is that they're both smart, accomplished, hardworking, and goal oriented. And yes, of course, wealthy. But they share another skill that most of us don't think about. Clinton and IBM chief Sam Palmisano are both very good at remembering people's names as soon as they're introduced. They embed them in their memories. Stories about this were legion when Clinton was on the campaign trail, and even on a White House receiving line. He had an uncanny ability to shake your hand, grasp your shoulder, say your name, and then commit it to memory. Palmisano, too, is well known in business circles—among employees of all levels—to recall someone's name, even if he met that person only once and didn't see him again until many months later. Palmisano started with IBM as a salesman and worked his way up through the ranks during the past three decades. Undoubtedly, meeting with customers helped him learn how to do this well, perhaps better than almost any other major CEO.

Most people admit that they're terrible at remembering names. And because most people aren't good at it, they assume it isn't a huge liability. In fact, they may be right. But being good at names can be a terrific plus, precisely because so many people don't do it. Most of us are flattered when a casual acquaintance, either in business or social circles, remembers our name. Just recently, I bumped into a man I hadn't seen in at least seven years. He had been an investor in my business, and then I somehow lost contact with him. I immediately said, "Rob, how are you? It's been a long time. How's Jill?" He was absolutely floored that I not only remembered his name, but his wife's, too. Rob called me and made a lunch date the very next day. (This is not an extremely difficult task. For many years, IBM salesmen kept detailed files on their customers; some even kept a database of the birthdays of their customers' spouses and children.)

You, too, can train yourself to remember names. It requires some work and some practice. Connect the face with the name in any way that works. Repeat it aloud, especially to get the pronunciation correct. "Jonathan Martin, is it? A pleasure to meet you." Or, say the name again slowly in your mind when you shake hands. Use mnemonic devices (memory devices)—i.e., think of someone you know by the same name. You've just met Jerry and he has monogrammed cufflinks, JPG. "Jerry—cufflinks." Alliteration often works well for some people. Robert has a ruddy face. "Robert—red." Catherine has long, curly hair. "Catherine—curls." Charles was complaining about a pain in his hamstring from too much tennis. "Charlie—horse." There are any number of devices you can use to imprint these new contacts in your mind. Find one that works for you, and practice it until you begin to remember with whom you just had a wonderful conversation only five minutes ago.

The best place to practice your name-memory exercises is in real time at cocktail parties or charity events. Put a certain number on your calendar every month, and make sure you turn your meet-and-greet time into a useful meet-greet-and-remember event.

YOUR REPUTATION PRECEDES YOU
AND SUCCEEDS YOU

Recently, I went to a friend's birthday party in Miami Beach. There were more than two hundred people wandering around the room. In the crowd I spotted someone who looked familiar, but I couldn't quite recall from where—it obviously had been some time ago. I made my way over and I approached the man.

"Excuse me, you look familiar to me. Do I look familiar to you?"

He cautiously responded, "Yes."

"What's your name?"

He told me he was Bernie S. Now I vividly remembered, and it wasn't a pleasant memory.

When my partner and I started Mercury Capital, we did business with Bernie S. My partner's father had been investing with Bernie for a couple of years. He was funding residential mortgages in tertiary locations on Long Island. Marc Gleitman, my partner, and I were novices at that time, and we relied on Bernie for finding opportunities and servicing the mortgages for us. Initially we invested $2 million that Bernie allocated among fifteen different mortgages. I never really liked Bernie. I felt that his attire was all wrong. I was sensitive to his whole appearance, including the way he spoke. He looked and sounded like a con man. His analytical interpretation of the deal was very vague. He told me not to sweat the details, but I like the details. All those things were triggers to me. My gut reaction was negative. However, Marc's dad had only good things to say so I went against my instincts.

Bernie's assistant (Ivy) corresponded with the borrowers and reported to me. The nature of this business includes servicing the mortgages, which requires calling the borrowers who are late and reminding them to pay. Bernie's assistant never gave me straight answers about the late payers. One day I decided to take over the servicing. I went into Marc's office and told him my intentions. I said I was going to send letters to all the mortgagors explaining that we own their mortgage and that in the future all the payments should be sent directly to Mercury Capital. I also told him that I was going to send these letters without informing Bernie.

Several days later one mortgagor called and said that he had paid off his mortgage six months ago. That seemed odd, since I had just received a payment on this mortgage two days earlier. Immediately, I realized what was happening. I ran into Marc's office and told him the story. He turned ashen.

Bernie had kept the $200,000 principal and continued to pay us interest as if the mortgage was still outstanding. Fortunately, we realized this early in our deal and after informing Bernie that we would turn the matter over to the district attorney, he paid us within a couple of weeks. Bernie created a classic Ponzi scheme, where the perpetrator keeps cashing the checks of unsuspecting people while paying off a certain amount of earlier debts—just enough to keep the scam going. Unfortunately, his other investors didn't fare as well as we did.

I had to refresh his memory; it had been a long time. "Bernie, don't you remember me? I am Jeffrey Meshel of Mercury Capital. When Marc Gleitman and I started our bridge loan business, we invested $2 million with you in various mortgages. Don't you remember what happened? I took over the servicing, and I discovered that one of the mortgages you were paying us on already had been paid off.

"Bernie, you tried to steal our money. In fact, we were lucky to find out when we did. However, I know a lot of other people that were not so lucky, including my partner's father. Bernie, didn't you also go to jail?"

> **Rule 5**
>
> The one thing you go to your grave with is your reputation. Guard it as you would guard anything you love dearly.

I told this story with five other people listening. Yes, the others were startled by my recitation of Bernie's infamous résumé. His hands started shaking, and he quietly walked away. The next day several people who heard what happened approached me. Not everyone would have done what I did. Yes, I did feel a sense of satisfaction in publicly humiliating and embarrassing this man. But I felt more obligated to let people know about this person's character and reputation. I wanted to make certain that Bernie—even though he's in a completely different field—isn't in a position to take advantage of other people.

When I've told others about this encounter, some people disagreed with my behavior, saying they would not have gone public. Perhaps you would have handled it differently. Put it this way: If a convicted rapist was living on your street, wouldn't you want every one of your neighbors to be aware of it? Perhaps mentioning in front of others could disabuse him of any notion to cause harm to another woman. Maybe not. But I stand by my methodology, even if others feel that I've overreacted.

A bad reputation is like an infection—it spreads very quickly, and worse, it stays with you forever. A good reputation takes years to build, and it can be destroyed in a day.

Here is another example, albeit less extreme. I've recently had the occasion to use a very high-powered real estate agent. He did an excellent job with a property I was involved with, absolutely first-rate. Because he is so good, I consistently began referring other people to him. What did I discover? He doesn't return their phone calls. So now I find myself still wanting to refer people to him, because I like him and I'm sure he's very good at what he does, but now I hedge my recommendation.

Typically, I'll say, "I'll be glad to recommend my agent, but I'll tell you up front, he's remiss about returning phone calls, and that's not good. That takes away his credibility." Now, the reason I frame it the way I do is that I don't want to diminish *my* credibility. The best thing that can happen is that if I refer someone to someone, they respond immediately. That enhances my reputation. If the person doesn't follow through, it lessens my reputation. So who am I going to be more inclined to refer, someone who's responsive or someone who's lax? If you build your team with people who are sensitive to each other, you should go out of your way to be responsive.

Remember, too, that your reliability speaks volumes about your reputation. Reliability can often trump the quality of work. Let's say you want to hire a contractor to redo your kitchen. It gets down to two quotes, almost exactly the same. One contractor's work is absolutely drop dead perfect, really unparalleled in materials and finishing. In fact, he's done some work that has made it into shelter magazines like *Architectural Digest*. The other isn't quite as dazzling, but he is very good nonetheless. You decide you like both, and you probably could close your eyes and just pick one. You do some due diligence and check with a half dozen references. You discover the first contractor—good as he is—is often late on jobs (he's so successful he's off bidding for new customers all the time), and almost always takes longer than he estimates to finish. The second guy, however, is absolutely true to his word. If he says his crew is coming at 8:00 A.M. on Friday, they're always there, promptly. Which one would you be inclined to hire?

Your word speaks more about your commitment and your reputation than the dozens of codicils and clauses on a written contract. That's for your lawyers—and theirs—to argue over when things get out of hand. People in business do not necessarily blame others for contract language that favors one party or another. These things are important, but they are not what begins and ends a deal. It's the handshake, the look in the eye that says you're honest, that you're trying to do business in a fair and equitable way, that you'll take the high road if it comes to a disagreement. It reflects your reputation.

3

Ask Not "What's in It for Me?"

The initial reaction to most requests is "What's in it for me?" It seems to be an instinct, almost a lesson that we are taught, and it's how 90 percent of the people you will come into contact with tend to manage their lives, both professionally and personally. It is selfish, and worse, a nearsighted approach to your business or career. I firmly believe you will become far more successful if you completely reverse this thinking and reeducate yourself. You will move further faster if you adjust your mind-set to first asking, "What can I do for you?" This is one of the major precepts of my philosophy, and it has worked amazingly well for the past two decades. Not only has it paid huge dividends for my business, it makes my day when I do an unsolicited favor for someone. It just feels great, and that's enough. It's a different kind of selfishness. It's become a prime motivation and one of my most effective networking mantras.

Most people are very impatient for reward. There are people who, no matter what they do for you, still have their hand out, always expecting something. I'll argue that in the end if you take the approach I suggest it will come back to you in ways you can never imagine. And your perception is different; your appreciation for the other party is different. People don't automatically have their defenses up if you don't expect an immediate quid pro quo. More opportunities will come your way if you're helping other people. It becomes a self-fulfilling prophecy.

My radar is always on. Whenever I meet a new client and explain the scope of the opportunities in our business, I always ask him to tell me about his business. I carefully record this information in my database. I never know when I'll have the opportunity to offer to do a favor, including putting that person in touch with someone else.

> **Rule 6**
>
> Instant gratification feels good, but don't think that this reward is the only one to strive for. Concentrate instead on the long term. Plant a lot of seeds. They will turn into trees.

You might recall that a number of years ago long distance phone service was expensive. It was right after new federal laws were passed, and telecommunications began to break off into different pieces. Suddenly, deregulation had multiple carriers sprouting up, all competing for our business. I used to receive calls weekly from salesmen trying to get me to change my company's carrier for a supposedly better deal. The cold calls were incessant, time consuming, and annoying.

My company's long distance bill at that time was approximately $3,000 a month, and like many small businesses, focusing on our phone bill was low on my list of priorities.

It was commonly believed that the difference in rates was probably nominal, and the idea of switching to another carrier was at the very least an office disruption.

One day I was having dinner with a few friends, one of whom was in the telecom business. We started chatting, and my friend, Todd, told me that he was a master distributor for one of the major carriers. This status gets his clients preferred pricing.

According to him, there were a limited number of master distributors and because of the amount of business they controlled, they had the best rates available. Todd offered to review my bill to see if he could do better for me. No charge, he insisted. You have no risk at all. Consider it a favor. Obviously, it was a smart business move to offer to look at my bill for free, especially since he was confident he could better my rate. While I stored away the information, I still really wasn't that interested. As much as I liked and respected Todd, I didn't expect to make a change. It was not something that I felt compelled to do anything about. I did the polite thing, and I told him I'd think about it.

During the next month, I continued to receive more solicitation calls to switch my phone service. Finally, somewhat exasperated, I called Todd and asked him if he would review my bill. He did. A week or so later, he called and promised that he could reduce my bill from $3,000 a month to about $1,300 a month. I was shocked. I couldn't believe the dramatic difference in rates—less than half what I was accustomed to paying—and suggested that we meet. I needed to understand how this worked.

Todd and I spent a couple of hours together. The explanation was pretty simple: The volume he controlled enabled him to get the lowest price. Clearly, if I was overpaying so was almost everybody else and, probably just like me, not focusing on it. I made the switch, and I never looked back. But also I thought this might be a wonderful opportunity to bring value to others I knew in my business orbit.

So I decided to spend a morning making some calls to "extend" this favor. I contacted a client who was in the paper business. Tom's company had ten locations situated all over the country, and I correctly surmised that he had to have a fairly hefty long distance phone bill, certainly bigger than mine. He was happy to hear from me, but then I immediately shifted gears, and asked, "Tom, I'm just curious, how large is your long distance phone bill?"

"Why?" he wondered. I related the experience I had with Todd and the amount of the savings that I began reaping.

"I would guess that my bill is around $30,000 a month."

"Tom, if you'd like, I could have Todd give you a call."

His initial response was pretty much as I suspected it would be—just like mine, a lukewarm reaction.

"I appreciate it, Jeff, but we've been using MCI for a long time and I know they treat me well. I just don't believe it will be worthwhile." (Now think about his response. This is not unlike a sales situation. I know I wasn't selling him anything; I was only trying to do a friend a favor. He did not say no; the door was ajar. Sometimes even when you simply want to help someone, you have to apply your best sales techniques.)

"Tom, the pivotal word in what you just said is 'believe,'" I countered. "Wouldn't you rather be sure that you are getting the best price? What's your downside? The guy doesn't charge anything to review your bill."

Tom paused and said just about the only thing he could say: "You're right. Have him give me a call."

About a month later, I heard from Tom. The conversation went something like this.

"Jeff, what's your favorite restaurant? I want to take you and your wife out for dinner."

"Why?"

"I could shoot myself. Your friend Todd did the review. He's able to knock my bill down from $30,000 a month to $16,000. I've been overpaying by $14,000 a month. That's $175,000 a year. I can't thank you enough."

The dinner was fine, by the way, but the personal satisfaction I received from creating value for his business left a far sweeter taste in my mouth.

But let's continue for a moment to look at what actually occurred with a more practical analysis. By making this introduc-

> **Rule 7**
>
> Share unrelated values and opportunities. Your relationships will appreciate it, and loyalties will grow.

tion, how is it valuable for me? I totally transformed my relationship with Tom, having become one of his trusted advisors. This occurred because I brought him additional value outside the parameters of my business. It is a classic example of not just "thinking out of the box" (the corporate cliché du jour) but of actually "*working* out of the box." (I'll discuss this in more detail later in the book.)

Prior to my helping him with his phone bill, Tom had never introduced me to anyone. I never asked him, and he never offered. Since the introduction to Todd, Tom has made it his priority to introduce me to several people, many of whom have become clients of my firm.

When you find something that has value, why not share it? It doesn't cost you anything. Sometimes I do this just because I like talking with my friends and business contacts. I'll use the flimsiest excuse to call. Say there's a sample sale; I've just discovered they're selling Burberry clothing or some name-brand clothing that's normally $100 and it's marked down to $30. I'll make calls to some friends just to let them know that it's there.

Since I travel extensively to Miami, I learned about a special offer that American Airlines was promoting. Occasionally, they have very good deals, but you have to know about them. This particular special offered a free round-trip plane ticket if you took two flights during a certain time period, between February and April. You could only take advantage of this offer twice. It was an excellent deal, and I immediately took advantage of it.

It didn't take long for me to begin thinking about all the people

I know who do the same thing that I do, because I have several contacts in my database whom I met on airplanes or in airport lounges. So I called up a friend of mine who's an executive at Bank of America, and I told him.

"You're kidding me," he said. "I didn't know about it. That's great." He called up and took advantage of the offer. And I called another fellow, and they were both very appreciative.

I extend this generosity to casual acquaintances and to people I don't even know. This may seem extreme to you, but again I always go to the extreme. Once when I was at the airport, I saw a man I see all the time on my flight but have never met. I walked over to him and said, "Excuse me, I'm sorry to bother you. I've seen you often, and I'm sure you've seen me; we seem to be taking the same flight." I wondered if he knew about the ticket promotion. He said, "Thank you so much. That's really nice of you to come over and tell me that. I didn't know about it." So we started talking, he gave me his business card, and now he's in my database. When he sees me in the airport terminal, he always says hello. It is a relationship that is beginning, and neither of us knows where it will lead, but that is not the point. The point is that I helped someone, and he was appreciative.

EXTREME THINKING CAN FOSTER EXTREME PAYOFFS

In 1996, I was introduced to an attorney, Robert, who thought well of my marketing skills. Robert later called me and asked if I could do him a favor. He asked me to read a new marketing piece he was about to print that was designed to troll for new business for his law firm. I was flattered that he asked my opinion and asked him to send it over immediately.

Over the weekend I read the text, and I was a little surprised at how poor the presentation was. The writing was not always clear, and it was obvious that it needed a lot of work. Now, most people who would have accepted the offer that I did would have merely done a cursory read and sent Robert back to the computer with some minor, gentle criticism that would not wound his ego.

I had a different take. I was in the middle of watching a football game, and during half time, I began editing the content. I was so absorbed with his material that I forgot about the game. In just a few hours, I ended up rewriting the entire piece. Some may wonder why I'd devote so much time to this. I'm not a professional editor, and I certainly wasn't being paid. On Monday morning, I called Robert. I was actually a little concerned that he might be offended by my taking the assignment too seriously.

"Robert," I began. "I hope you don't get annoyed with me. I read your brochure and started to make changes. In fact, I changed most of it." Bob is not an insecure man, however, and I should have realized that he would not have a problem with my marking up his work.

"Jeff, please send it to me," he said. "I would really like to see what you did."

Robert loved my changes. A week or two later, he called and asked if I had any interest in buying an apartment. It turns out he was the president of his co-op board, and there was a great opportunity to buy a penthouse in his building. He was totally up front about the problems. The apartment was in sorry shape, in fact, a complete fixer-upper, but it was quite large, about 2,600 square feet. My wife and I immediately put in a lowball offer of $260,000. An estate owned the property, and the grandchildren were anxious to sell it. And because it needed so much work, it had attracted few offers. My timing was apparently good because, after a minimum of negotiation, my offer was accepted. Robert expedited my board approval (and asked me to join the board right away). It took a year to renovate the place, and I spent $400,000 getting it into really livable shape. We enjoyed living there for nearly three years, and when we decided to move, we sold it for $1.9 million.

So the two and a half hours I spent working on Robert's marketing piece eventually netted me a profit of more than $1 million. It probably never would have happened if I hadn't done Robert that favor. Now, I obviously didn't know when I was sitting there watching a weekend football game, making the changes, that I would reap this kind of reward. The opportunity occurred because I simply decided to go out of my way for someone I liked.

Now, a word of caution. Do not expect your largesse to always produce satisfactory results. I can think of instances where I continually helped a person and the situation turned sour. It is not uncommon for someone I've helped to suddenly notice one of the transactions I'm doing and call to say, "You know, I have somebody who would be interested in this." I'll eagerly reply, "Oh, that's great, thank you. By all means, please have him call me, or if you'd like I'll call him." Then this person says, "Is there a referral fee?" My red flag goes up. He's making this call not to help me but because he's thinking, "What's in it for me?" My reply? I simply tell him we do not pay referral fees.

Now my perception of this man immediately changes. I've gone out of my way numerous times, and I never asked for anything in return. I will probably think twice the next time I'm in a position to help him because he's suggested our relationship is based on his avarice. He's interested only in increasing his bottom line and not really about building a solid relationship. And that's as far as it goes. I'll likely not hear from this person again.

I'm always improving my networking skills, almost to the point where I don't even realize I'm *actually* networking. I forget that I'm doing some good for someone, because I like doing it. By doing this, I become empowered. I sense that people now perceive me more positively because I go out of my way to network. People with business vacuums or problems will commonly say, "Oh, you've got to call Jeff. Jeff will know someone who can help you." This type of reaction snowballs and accelerates.

So don't ask what someone can do for you, ask what you can do for someone else. Be a facilitator. In the end, it comes back.

4

Perception of Self
How Others See You

I serve on several advisory boards, and on one of those boards, the chairman of the firm and I have become very good friends. Often we get together for dinner and discuss current business issues and opportunities that his firm is engaging in. It isn't unusual for me to speak with him several times a day. When he calls me, I try to take his call immediately, yet when I call him his secretary picks up and typically asks me if I can hold. He rarely picks up quickly. "He'll be with you in a moment" is the common refrain.

Nine out of ten times I am on hold for an extended period of time. Now when I call, I watch the timer on my phone and, when it hits two minutes, I just hang up. Who hasn't heard this tune before, especially among contacts you do business with regularly, and for whom you otherwise have a high regard?

Early in our relationship I used to get annoyed, thinking his behavior was very rude. Picture this: I am intimately involved in the day-to-day operations of his firm, and he isn't immediately responsive to my calls. If he is tied up, which is understandable, why doesn't he simply instruct his secretary to say he'll get back to me? This is not rocket science in the world of manners. It's common courtesy.

What is the reaction when a first-time caller is left on hold for an extended period of time? It is virtually guaranteed that the first impression will be negative. Arrogance, rudeness, thoughtlessness are just some impressions a person waiting might have.

I'm in a situation now with someone I've done a business deal with, and I've been in the position to potentially refer several people to him. But I've noticed his phone manners are wanting. In his case, he is remiss when it comes to returning a phone call. Now, what if I tell someone to call, and that person leaves a message and there is no returned call? Not only is my referral unimpressed but he's also probably wondering why I recommended him. What's worse is that my credibility is potentially diminished, and I will think very hard about making any other referrals to him unless they are qualified. That means I may say something like, "I'll be glad to introduce you to him, but he is a little quirky. He isn't great about returning phone calls." If he can't return a phone call, how well can he execute his business?

Since it's obvious that this type of behavior offends people, why do it?

> **Rule 8** Wake up! Be aware of what you do or don't do and how those affected will react.

The explanation is different for different people. In the case of my friend, he is just oblivious, and he isn't thinking about the person on hold. He literally doesn't realize what he's doing. For many executives they're flexing their fragile egos by exercising the control they perceive they have. Don't take it personally; they just don't care.

I have another friend who worked most of his life for large public companies. I mentioned this man's habit of leaving me on hold or not returning my calls. He said that in corporate America this type of behavior is more common than most people think. Rudeness is the norm. If you demand an immediate response, you are fooling yourself. He said to exercise patience. They expect you to grovel, especially if they perceive that you need them more than they need you. It's a silly little power play exercised by executives and others who are, at their core, incredibly insecure.

Many of these people have low self-esteem, or feel they are underpaid and look to exhibit power wherever they can. The reality is that they would be better off building as many relationships and friendships as possible because as we all know corporations tend to go through periods where large numbers of people are systematically laid off. In today's fast-moving, volatile economy, sooner rather than later, many of those who wield the power will find themselves on the other end. They'll be terminated and hope someone else will be in a position to help. I wonder how they'll feel if nobody returns their calls. Sherry Lansing, a powerful Hollywood studio executive, makes certain she returns everyone's calls within twenty-four hours. Would it surprise you to learn that she's been at the head of Paramount longer than any other current studio head? If she can do it, so can you.

> **Rule 9**
>
> Leo Durocher, the legendary baseball manager, once said, "Nice guys finish last." He had it wrong: Nice guys finish first.

So, what to do about my friend, the chairman, who was constantly leaving me dangling at the end of my telephone cord? One evening while I was having dinner with him, I decided to broach the touchy subject of his phone habits. I never directly confront someone with his or her problem, however. I tend to go deeper, trying to unmask the psychology behind the behavior.

PERCEPTION OF SELF—NOT SELF-PERCEPTIONS

I began by asking him a somewhat disarming question: "Do you know what perception of self is?" He thought for a moment and answered, "Is it how I perceive myself?"

I said, "No, to the contrary. Actually it is being aware and sensitive to how the person you are interacting with perceives you. Let me give you an example. When I call your office and you leave me on hold, are you sensitive to the fact that I am sitting there waiting for you to finish your call? I know that when I receive a call and I am on the other line, I am really uncomfortable about leaving somebody on hold for anything other than a brief period of time—fifteen or twenty seconds even seems long. In fact, if my existing conversation runs longer than a short interval, I excuse myself for a moment and pick up the party on hold just to ask them if I can call them back shortly. Many times when I call you I'm on hold for three or four minutes and ultimately just hang up. You probably are not even conscious that I was there, or that I became intolerant waiting. I am sure that I'm not the only person you do this to. Someone who isn't your friend or close to you could easily be offended or just think you are arrogant, neither of which is the message you want to send. I think it is extremely important that you are always conscious of the way people perceive you."

My friend listened and, to his credit, acknowledged that I was right. He committed to managing this aspect of his business, and I decided to test the results the next day. I called my friend and I was only on hold for fourteen seconds. The chairman has since become a more thoughtful respondent. I hope he is doing the same with others.

"Perception of self" is an essential awareness. I know that when I meet someone new, I control his or her perception of me. I feel empowered by this. I convey enthusiasm and sincerity. Most important, I am knowledgeable. Based on the reactions I receive, I sense a positive perception from my initial meetings.

When you finish a first meeting with someone, do you feel that the person you spoke with is interested in you and what you do? Did you impress them? Do they like you? Did you have their attention? Any product or service that you are selling starts with whether you are positively perceived.

Think about these points for a moment. People buy, invest, in people.

Recently, I introduced an early-stage (pre-revenue) telecom company to an entrepreneur in transition. I thought there might be a good match. Steve is an accomplished businessman who began his career at one of the major telecoms and worked his way up to become the right-hand man to the president and CEO. He went on to start several successful technology-based companies and ultimately took them to the point where he created some modest capital. He was now looking for his next opportunity.

He was extremely intrigued by the company's business model and anxious to be involved. During the first couple of weeks Steve would call me many times each day to discuss the opportunity and what I thought the company's reactions were to him being part of their team. Our conversations became so analytical that I was wondering if he was too anxious. The irony is that for the fifteen years I have known Steve his analytical intensity has annoyed me on many occasions. I think his business career has suffered from this problem. Still, Steve is very smart and could potentially be the missing component on the executive team of the new company.

A meeting was scheduled to discuss the company's financial needs and his potential role. The day before the meeting Steve was pacing in my office and asked my opinion of what he was going to say. "How does this sound?" he asked. "Dave, did you speak to your partners more about my involvement? I know that I can roll out this product nationwide. I am ready to start right away and . . ."

I immediately cut him off.

"Steve, stop. You are being way too pushy. You sound desperate. Relax. Let them come to you a little bit. You have the right credentials, and they know it. You don't want them to perceive desperation. Reverse the roles. Let them convince you to be a part of the company. They know you are the missing piece." I suggested that he tell them: "I'm very interested in the business. I've done all the due diligence, and I may be ready to make a commitment. However, things are still in an early stage and the market is difficult, and I'd like to hear what some of your ideas are involving strategy and the competition."

In his initial approach, Steve looked like he was hungry for a job. When this occurs, you devalue your assets. The other side then begins thinking they have the wrong person, they may have aimed too low, or, at the minimum, their negotiating prowess is enhanced.

With the second approach Steve is asking them to sell him on joining their team.

Credibility is an essential part of how you are ultimately perceived. In my core business, on a daily basis I am presented with opportunities to finance transactions that need to close immediately. These transactions are normally secured by real estate. So brokers constantly pitch me with new deals. Some recent examples illustrate the range of trust and respect I would give to two different brokers.

In the first one, a mortgage broker called me about a Key Biscayne home that was up for sale. He briefly explained the particulars. It was a third mortgage on a very expensive home in a very exclusive neighborhood. The house was worth $15 million, and the first and second mortgages totaled $8.9 million. That left approximately $6 million of equity in the house, and because the owner was going through a divorce, he needed an additional $2 million. The owner was a successful lawyer, and he was trying to stave off a foreclosure. Even if he sold the house in a distress sale for $11 million my investment would be protected.

Well, briefly, this wasn't a transaction that I was very interested in. It was, however, a high-profile piece of real estate so I made one call and in five minutes I got the real story. I found out it wasn't worth anywhere near $15 million. In fact, six months ago they had had an auction in the house, where one hundred people showed up on the lawn, and the starting bid was $12 million, and no one bid for it. The prominent lawyer was indeed going through a divorce, but the broker neglected to mention that his client was being prosecuted for absconding with money from his clients' escrow accounts. Now either the broker was incredibly inept or he was outright lying. I assumed he knew the house's history. He didn't really care whether I made a good or bad loan. I didn't think he was inept, but he withheld that information, and, in fact, he totally portrayed a completely different scenario. So immediately, he has zero credibility. I know never to consider anything he says as having a basis in fact.

Coincidentally, right about the time that deal was offered to me, another broker made an appointment with me to propose another deal. He came to my office with a very thorough package, told me a very precise story about a transaction in Puerto Rico. I asked to meet with the principal, who gave me the exact same story. They had all the details, all the backup data, and nearly all of my questions answered before I asked them. Then the broker said, "There are a couple of issues you should know about," and he just laid out all the risks, all the possible encumbrances. Now, I'm interested in this transaction. I'll do some more due diligence before making a decision. Already, I respect this broker. He's given me the perception that he's credible. If someone calls me and says to me, "Do you know this guy?" I'm going to say you should hear him out. He's a sharp guy, on his game, and he says it the way it is. And that's worth a lot.

Perception of self is probably one of the most important barometers of awareness. Ask yourself these key questions:

> ➤ How do people who you know perceive you?
> ➤ How do new introductions react to you?
> ➤ Are you viewed as smart and sharp at what you do?
> ➤ Are you viewed as a giver or as a taker?
> ➤ Do others *think* you are connected?
> ➤ Are you well liked by your peers; are you viewed as a good person?
> ➤ Do people respect your opinion?
> ➤ Are you honest and sincere?
> ➤ Do you follow through with what you say you are going to do?
> ➤ Do you take the lead in conversations?
> ➤ Are you ever overbearing or overanxious when making a point?

It is sometimes hard to be objective when taking a self-examination quiz such as the one above. I liken it to the obvious job interview question when you're asked to describe your weak points or flaws. It's a purposely loaded question, because nobody any good will say they have none, even in jest. It requires taking a candid step back. If you have difficulty making an assessment, I suggest you ask someone you have a fairly intimate business relationship with to evaluate you. Ask him to be painfully honest. If he exposes the negatives, you know you have some personal work on your agenda, not to mention a real friend.

YOU ARE OFTEN PERCEIVED BY THE WAY YOU LOOK

Everyone has heard the story about how a hip young black man, dressed in the latest ghetto fashion—flashy sneakers, Lakers jersey, baggy three-quarter pants, ostentatious jewelry—walks into the local Bentley dealer. He spends five or ten minutes inspecting the high-priced cars, and he cannot get a salesman to wait on him. The showroom staff has no idea that he's a rap star, worth millions, probably would make an impulse buy for a car costing six figures, and pay cash—if only someone were merely attentive. Today, luxury car salesmen are a bit smarter. But it's a telling story about perception. Businessmen wearing Armani suits with expensive cuff links and silk ties are fawned over, even if they have no intention of buying. The perception may be wrong, but this is the reality of things.

I have a friend who has a successful pension-consulting business. When I first met him, he had just a small actuarial shop, and I wondered why a guy who seemed to have so much going for him wasn't doing a bigger business. The first thing I noticed was that his buttoned-down shirt had a frayed collar. Now, this in itself is not a particularly big thing. But the frayed collar distracted me enough to begin inspecting his entire wardrobe. His suit was not pressed, and, when I looked closer, it seemed outdated. The material was a cotton and polyester blend, not wool. His socks clashed with his suit. Normally, I'm not a snob about how expensively someone dresses. Plenty of people on a budget know how to coordinate clothes and put together an outfit that looks good.

My take in short? A nice enough guy, but a lousy dresser in a profession where conventional business dress is expected. Did the clothes make the man? Obviously not. A bad perception, however, can scotch a deal. And trust me, it can begin with a frayed collar.

I made a superficial judgment dictated by his shabby appearance. My perception, like narrow-minded luxury car salesmen, was wrong. Over time I began to realize the quality of his character and how smart he truly was. We served on a board together and after two years or so, it became obvious that the one thing he didn't focus on was his attire. His suits were old and poorly fitting. His shirts and ties were unfashionable. I'm not suggesting that he was inappropriate; he just didn't have perception of self in this regard. He didn't see what others saw.

This man heads a financial services company, and one of his primary functions is to bring in new business. As we became good friends, I ultimately felt comfortable enough to talk to him about his appearance. One night over dinner I said, "David, I want to tell you something. I want you to understand that you are my dear friend and my comments are intended to be constructive.

"You are the president of your company, so you are also the rainmaker. When you sell your services, think about whom you are speaking to, the president, the CFO, or the owner of the company. You are trying to convince these people to hire you to manage some of their most important assets, often millions of dollars. You are asking owners of companies to trust you with their pensions.

"But your clothing looks like it was acquired at the Salvation Army. You look impoverished. If someone is going to trust you with the company retirement plan, don't you think you need to *look* successful? Even if I thought you were brilliant, there is a limited possibility that I would not give you my assets to invest. You need to dress the part. Here's what I would like you to do. Come with me and get some custom-made shirts and new suits. Trust me. Look at it as an investment that will pay dividends."

After a few weeks of prodding, David took my advice. He

looked great with the wardrobe makeover. He admitted the new clothes made him *feel* confident. His self-esteem got a lift as well. His business has improved dramatically, and so has the way that others perceive him.

> **Rule 10**
>
> The perception may be wrong, but it doesn't matter. Perception is reality.

A lot of people are not cognizant of the way someone sees them. They just aren't sensitive to the reaction that a person has to them. Often, it comes down to looking in someone's eyes. When you look in someone's eyes, you can tell whether you have them engaged or not.

There is a list of things to be mindful of that can create a negative perception. If you meet someone who has discolored teeth that really stand out, it subliminally creates a bad impression. Sometimes it isn't even subliminal. I'm actually turned off to someone like that on a certain level. Why? Because on a certain level, lack of good hygiene is a turnoff. And I'm a curious type. I think, this person is driving a Mercedes, takes off whenever he wants to play golf during the week, and obviously has the money to have his teeth fixed. Is there some reason why he doesn't? Is he out of touch? Or just doesn't care?

> **Rule 11**
>
> Drive yourself to be better—every day.

A colleague told me a story about how his close friend from high school sent his daughter to have breakfast with him. This woman was a newly minted Ivy League graduate, top grades, obviously intelligent and ambitious. She was searching for a job in politics, and my colleague was very well connected, having worked for some influential public figures. He was very impressed with her, but one thing bothered him. During conversation with her, he noticed she had a tongue stud, and this kind of ornament can be very distracting. He told me, "I respected her right to wear body jewelry, but I told her father the truth. I couldn't comfortably recommend her to the kinds of people who were in a position to hire her. They would be totally turned off."

Now, since this woman is obviously high caliber in every respect, she could have the attitude that suggests, "This is who I am, and if you can't handle this part of my appearance, then you're someone who I don't want to work for anyway." If this is true, then it's an arrogant pose. If she is simply ignorant and unaware of the impression she's making, then it's up to another adult to clue her in. Whatever the reason, her appearance is not good. She has to be informed that her look is offensive to a lot of people within the business she's attempting to penetrate.

This just means you should be mindful of presenting yourself in the best possible way you can. You cannot skimp when it comes to your attire, and, of course, you should choose your accessories wisely. Buy clothes that make you look as presentable as possible. Because the first thing someone sees is your physical appearance. They have an immediate reaction. They draw an instant conclusion, fair or unfair, right or wrong. That's reality. And if you can put yourself in the most advantageous position with that first perception, it's going to pay dividends.

To summarize, it's crucial that you are on top of the way you look, the way you sound, and the way you present yourself. The smallest detail can put somebody off, and people in business have remarkable memories. You will continually run across someone who cannot deal with someone else for the pettiest reason. It's illogical, I know, but this is the way the world works.

Again, be sure you ask yourself: Are you cognizant of the way people are perceiving you? When you're speaking, does the person listening think you're smart? Do you have their attention? Just how well are you engaging them? Do they respond to you in a way that says you control the conversation? Do you feel that person is energized by you?

If I'm in control of a conversation and I know a person is responding to me, it gives me a good deal more confidence. If I think the person likes me, I know I have them. You can do this, too.

5

Dealing with Shyness
How to Overcome It

If you do a Google search on the Internet and type in the word "shyness," you will find approximately 307,000 pages linked to your request. Studies have concluded that one in fifteen people experiences panic attacks induced by a social phobia—some type of shyness or anxiety—when circulating among strangers. I am amazed how pervasive shyness is and how hindering it can be. It's a part of what mental health experts call social anxiety disorder, and it's an affliction that is taken very seriously. There are already drugs being tested in clinical trials to treat shyness disorders. If your problem is more than the common butterflies most of us endure, then you should consider seeking professional help. It will likely do some good. In most cases, however, shyness is not a life sentence.

I was amazed, when discussing this topic, how many of my friends consider themselves to be shy. My friend Hal told me that it took many years for him to overcome shyness. Hal is now incredibly outgoing. When I polled my colleagues, they said I'd be doing readers a disservice if I didn't discuss shyness and how to deal with it.

AN INTROVERT LOOSENS UP

My friend Sy Siegal is a living example of how a trend does not necessarily dictate one's destiny. His is a classic story of how he learned to become better at networking, despite the handicap of having a difficult time meeting new people.

As a teenager Sy was shy and awkward in social situations. Being overweight didn't help. Obviously, he had a bad perception of himself. He was the classic introvert off by himself when everybody else was out having a good time. He had friends but he wasn't one of the kids you'd call popular. Fortunately, Sy wasn't lazy. He worked very hard in the classroom, and he always had an after-school job. He became manager of a retail store (probably one of the best learning jobs you can have, as I mentioned earlier) while going to school as a full-time student.

Sy Siegal attended City College of New York (once known as the "poor man's Harvard"), populated by typically lower-middle-class students who were the brightest, hardest-working kids around. Often they were the first generation in this country and had graduated from the local public high schools, a diverse but ultimately homogenous group. There, Sy hit another stumbling block. He developed a stutter. "It just sort of appeared in my later college years," he recalled. "I had a problem with the what, why, when, where, the 'wh.' I just couldn't get the word out. It wasn't severe, and I didn't think much of it. It was probably a result of my anxiety about the future."

Fortunately, a friend of Siegel's invited him to a meeting of the New York Republican Club. He had a passion for politics and government and spent hours listening to public servants on talk radio. He got involved with his peers who worked on the John Lindsay mayoral campaign. There, he was exposed to people from several different levels of affluence. Some attended private schools or out-of-town colleges; some were economically advantaged; and others worked for white-shoe law firms and prestigious businesses.

He became active in various election campaigns and eventually became president of what was then an important political club that had some very well-known, well-connected people. "I was able to learn how the world of politics worked," Siegal told me. "Many of my fellow club members went on to high-powered careers in government and business." Over the years, these relationships facilitated business opportunities that would not have evolved if he hadn't participated. All that time he was networking and he didn't even realize it.

He gained a load of experience interacting with customers, and today he enjoys spending time with his many long-term clients. But it took a long time for him to emerge from his shell, and it also took some proactive work on his part. Thankfully, his industrious nature helped him overcome what can be severe impediments in business.

From that experience he absorbed an important truth. You could succeed if you were willing to work hard. This was the great equalizer, the antidote, if you will, to money and bloodline. But it's only when he combined all this with newly learned networking skills that Siegal was able to fulfill his potential.

The time he spent working with political wonks helped him elevate his self-esteem, reduced his anxiety, and just as suddenly as his stutter appeared, it miraculously disappeared. Looking back, he said it also gave him the courage, at age twenty-six, to start his own business, an accounting firm. He had such an urge to control his own destiny that it was a logical step to take. The entrepreneur wears many hats, and one of them is surely sales and marketing, which became his prime role. "I understood early on that the key to building my business was in both developing personal relationships and constantly networking," he said. "This is no easy task for shy people."

Siegal is now involved with many philanthropic and business boards. "There were many occasions where I was a dinner chairman or honoree," he said. "And there were many times that I was called on to make a speech. To the shy person this can be a horrifying experience. But I was generally able to employ some relaxation techniques that helped me get through the most difficult moments."

Today, he explains how he continually works at the problem. "There are a number of things I do," he explained. "I locate somebody in the room that I might know. That person will get me warmed up. Once I get warmed up, I focus on one individual I don't know yet. I try to strike up a conversation with that one person, then I can proceed. It's the first encounter that's very difficult and key. So it's helpful when people use name tags. I always found that I'm no different from 90 percent of the people in the room. They want to talk to me as much as I want to talk to them.

"Even to this day, as confident as I am, when I enter a room full of strangers I literally stand at the doorway, frozen, summoning up whatever techniques might work to get me in that room. I still battle it, and I try all kinds of tricks to overcome it," he said. "I do a pretty good job, but it's not something that's gone away completely. It's chronic, like an illness you can control but really can never completely cure."

The most important lesson he learned was that most people were in the same awkward position as he was. So you work the room and you collect some business cards. When the time for the follow-up call comes, you have to overcome your shyness once more. Remember, everybody at one point asks themselves these questions: Did he or she like me? How serious was he when he suggested getting together for lunch? Was he just being polite?

When you're shy this can be an excruciatingly painful experience. It requires some courage to take the next step and make that call.

> **Rule 12**
>
> Shyness may be a personality characteristic, but it need not be lifelong. If you're shy, work to overcome it.

Like almost anyone else, I had a pretty significant degree of shyness at some point. And by challenging myself, I completely overcame it. And now I don't feel that I'm really shy at all. I suppose I am lucky. I can strike up a conversation anywhere, anytime. I fly frequently, shuttling between New York and Miami and wherever my business happens to take me. If I'm in an airport and we're sitting in the lounge waiting to board a plane, I have no problem talking to the person right next to me. He's casually reading the sports page, and I'll notice what story he's reading and comment on it. If there's a delay, I can start with the most mundane of subjects—the weather. It doesn't take long for me to find out what he does for a living. People are often struck by how after only ten or fifteen minutes with a total stranger, I'm exchanging business cards with him, even though my intent has nothing to do with business.

I read four newspapers a day because I want to know what's going on out there. I hunger for knowledge, and my appetite is never sated. If somebody brings up something in current events, I'm aware of it. It's a great way to get talking and draw someone in. For example, you could say, "Did you hear what happened at Bloomingdale's today? They had the store all cordoned off; there was a terrorist threat." Suddenly, you start having a conversation about something that anyone can relate to. Before long, they ask, "What do you do?" And that opens the door to a conversation. So you can take items or props and use them to open a conversation. And you just start chatting.

I'm now more secure in what I know, and this is really the crux of overcoming shyness.

Remember that self-doubt and shyness go hand in hand. If you don't feel good about yourself or if you are not sure of yourself, then you will become more introverted. Sometimes there is a chain reaction, which can lead to depression.

Don't confuse shyness with laziness. There is a side to this issue that says, "I just don't want to do it." When I'm at a business cocktail party, I want to enjoy myself, but I consider it work. I've got to expend energy, and I've got to make myself gregarious and persuade myself to be talkative and curious. Some people just don't want to do it. They claim they're shy. But is it shyness? Or lack of discipline? I'll argue that they are linked to some degree. If you're lazy you might think, "I'm just going to go get a drink and stand in the corner because I'm shy." I would re-examine that explanation. Maybe you're not shy. Maybe you're lazy and you just don't feel like doing the work. If you truly don't feel like working the room, then don't go to the cocktail party. You'll only make a poor impression. If you're in a bad mood, forget it—don't even bother going to the cocktail party. If your mood is somber or you're bothered by something important, you're not going to have the energy to do the work. You won't be at your best, and your mood will show.

The saddest part about shyness in the business world is not the discomfort it causes those afflicted, but the opportunities that are missed by sitting back in meetings and silently watching as colleagues speak up and reap their rewards while the shy guy is still formulating his or her thoughts. Overcoming shyness in the business world is hard. It requires all the skills necessary to overcome shyness in other areas of our life and more. Not only must we be able to carry on a conversation with others at a moment's notice but we must also be able to do it under pressure in an interview, during a sales pitch, or on a cold call.

From networking to public speaking, shyness stunts our growth because it keeps us from learning the things we need to know to do our jobs well.

Salespeople, the group of people who most need to have an outgoing nature and confidence, spend more time and money developing these skills than any other group. (Charisma, on the other hand, is an innate characteristic.)

The question is what can you do to combat shyness and be more assertive. You have to challenge yourself; you have to make yourself better. It's a discipline like anything else. If you find that you're in the crowded room, why did you go there? You went there to meet some new people, perhaps somebody who will be worthwhile knowing in business. And yet you get there, and you don't do it. So you have to motivate yourself and say, "I'm going to make myself do it. I'm going to push myself to do it." Sometimes you have to force yourself to engage in a conversation.

Rule 13

Don't change *who you are,* change the way you *think.*

Here are some helpful steps toward building self-confidence and overcoming shyness:

➤ Recognize your strengths and weaknesses as they relate to your personality. As self-acceptance grows, shyness naturally diminishes. Maximize your strengths and chip away at your weaknesses.

➤ There are numerous approaches to every problem and issue. Few opinions are completely right or wrong. Don't be afraid to speak up and voice your viewpoint. In fact, push yourself to share your opinions.

➤ Your success as a businessman or entrepreneur hinges on how well you communicate with people. Therefore, set clear goals in what you want to accomplish. Practice articulating your pitch, even in front of colleagues who can offer advice and criticism.

➤ Turn your focus away from yourself when you're at a networking event. Instead of feeling embarrassed about forcing yourself onto the other person, simply switch the focus of the conversation to that person.

➤ Do not be afraid to ask very direct, pertinent, conversation-starting questions, for example: Are you a member? Are you a member of other organizations like this one? How do they compare? How have you benefited from your membership? Do you attend meetings regularly? Have you received business or benefits by participating? What business are you in?

The irony is that when you allow people to talk about themselves, they'll be more likely to enjoy the conversation with you and naturally view your business in a positive light. They don't know they're doing you a service by getting you to relax, be yourself, and overcome your shyness. This helps in many ways. You'll be indirectly promoting yourself and your business without selling to the other person. Also, after you've met someone new, you can take it upon yourself to introduce that person to others—yet another shyness inhibitor.

You can reduce your level of shyness by noting the following tips:

➤ Continually refine your speaking skills. The ability to speak confidently and well is a talent universally admired and envied. If you have the opportunity to speak in front of a group, this is excellent experience.

➤ Force yourself to turn off the tube and read regularly. Become acquainted with several disciplines outside your direct line of work. When you are an authority on a subject, however esoteric, you will be respected and your confidence will increase.

➤ Learn to cope with disappointments and failures. Dwelling on them will turn you inward and won't help your outgoing self. Think positively. Often disappointment is a learning experience and becomes a springboard for a new opportunity.

➤ Repetition and drilling have an important place in your day. Practice the hard stuff—your pitches, your dialogue, your introductions to people you've never met. Do a dry run in front of a mirror. Put yourself on the receiving end of your presentation. Did you like it? Did you feel comfortable and confident? If not, keep practicing.

➤ Use devices that engage conversation whenever you can. Think how you would phrase a recent event prior to entering into the room, and you'll forget that you were feeling shy about meeting someone new. You'll be concentrating on asking someone what he thought of the event.

➤ Do not be afraid to disagree in a polite but forceful manner. You can support your opinion in an intelligent fashion. Just say, "I understand your point, and I appreciate it. But let me tell you why I think you're wrong." Or, "Let me explain my point of view." The first time you convince someone to change his mind, you will feel confident and overcome your shyness.

➤ Be involved in extracurricular activities—sports, hobbies— that you excel in. Your confidence will grow.

➤ Ask questions. I often do, especially when prominent

speakers open up the floor for a Q&A. Your mind should be working to prepare a provocative question, even before he finishes his speech. I was at a small fundraiser recently for a politician at a private residence, and after he was introduced and made a few remarks, I immediately asked him a precise question. This kind of interaction not only helps you overcome shyness but lets you stand out.

6

Basic Sales Tactics
Turn No into Maybe, Maybe into Yes

A good networker is also a good salesman. Networking and selling are irrevocably intertwined. I've rarely met anyone who was adept at one and not the other. And so it follows that the principles and characteristics that define excellence in both are very closely related. A salesman must be assertive but not overly aggressive. He must be confident but not presumptuous. He has to learn how to give more than he expects in return. He has to believe in what he is selling, and he has to maintain a high standard. The same is true for networking.

In 1985, when I was 28, I started my own company. That might not seem so bold today—technology start-ups are commonly run by younger people, even college students like Michael Dell—but twenty years ago, it wasn't an everyday occurrence. I'd like to report that this move was a carefully planned moment in my business career. But it wasn't. A colleague, Marc Gleitman, and I were working for a real estate syndicator. We didn't like the company's tactics; it had been engaging in numerous marginal and unscrupulous practices that we weren't aware of when we originally signed on. We could not in good conscience continue working there.

Our alternatives were either to find other jobs or to strike out on our own. Looking for a new job was not an attractive idea to me. Since we had both learned something about the real estate business, we decided to syndicate our own deal.

After several months of looking at various opportunities, Marc and I formed a company, AREC Real Estate, to acquire real property. (AREC stood simply for Another Real Estate Company. We wanted to be listed at the top of any directory so we picked an "A" name.) Our first transaction was simple but ambitious, at least for us. We were going to build six houses in Quogue, a town in Long Island's East End resort community. We found a home builder and negotiated a turnkey price of $260,000 for a 2,500-square-foot house. Everything would be included—a pool, hot tub, and tennis court—and each home would be situated on an acre and a half of land. With the second-home market in New York appearing to be robust, we expected to make a significant profit on each house. We also added what we thought was a clever addition to the deal. We would acquire a shopping center in Roanoke, Virginia, that was already built, which could spin off cash while we were waiting for the houses to be completed. This would require another $900,000 in capital.

We had to raise $2.2 million in cash, mainly through high net-worth investors. This task fell squarely on my shoulders. I had a lot of calls to make. I had to cast a very wide net.

There is an old saying that timing is everything, and in our maiden deal, it turned out that our timing couldn't have been worse. That year, in a somewhat surprising move, Congress modified the tax laws so that second-home purchases were less attractive for investors. While the proposed statute to disallow second-home mortgage deductions was defeated, there were other changes that made these investments more difficult to sell. This, combined with a strong dollar, increased travel abroad and exacerbated the negative perception of these properties. Our contract deposits had just gone "hard" maybe a week or so prior to the tax change announcement. So we couldn't back out without losing all the cash we'd already invested.

I sent out five hundred memorandums to prospective investors and only received one call. The one person who responded said, "Are you crazy, are you really going to try to do this?" I started to feel a little insecure, like I was trying to sell snowballs in the North Pole.

My partner and I had a small one-room office, smaller than the typically sized conference room, and our desks were catty-cornered to each other. Envision a single desk contiguous to Marc's contiguous to our secretary's desk. The three of us looked at each other all the time—and already after only a few months, we were in survival mode for our fledgling company. There was absolutely no interest. Failure loomed as a real possibility.

After a week of rejections, Marc asked me if I realistically thought we could raise the money. I turned and looked at him and said we had no choice. We *had* to get this deal done. Both of us literally had put all of our own money down to start this business. If we didn't close this transaction, we would be looking for jobs very shortly.

I continued making follow-up phone calls and each response was consistent. "Yes, Jeff, I looked at it, I'm really not interested." The reasons varied, but they all finished in the same place: "not interested."

KNOW THE DIFFERENCE BETWEEN A "HARD" NO AND A "SOFT" NO

A good salesman must distinguish the difference between a hard no and a soft no. I am continually surprised at how many people in the average sales force cannot do this. They drone on and on when they have absolutely no chance at all. When salespeople try to sell to me and I don't have any interest, I just interrupt the person and say, "Excuse me, I'll listen to whatever you have to say. I'm just telling you right now, I am not interested, and here are the reasons I'm not going to buy what you're selling. If you want to keep trying, I'll listen because I'm polite—not receptive—polite. But I'm just telling you up front so that you *don't* waste your time." This is a hard no, and a good salesman would pack up his briefcase and move on to the next potential customer.

Often, people will not be as forthcoming as I am. So you have to understand that people will shrug and fidget and not exactly say no when they are, in effect, never going to waver and change their minds. People have a difficult time saying no because no means rejection, and since they've been rejected themselves, they know how painful it sometimes is. People generally don't want to inflict pain on others, especially if the salesman is cheerful, polite, and nice.

That said, a series of continual no-thank-yous has to be carefully evaluated. It is not automatically a signal to simply give up. Constant rejection can reflect on the quality of the product or service you're offering, but more often it has more to do with a faulty approach. In the case of the first deal we did, I remained fully convinced the problem was with my sales pitch.

After several weeks of constant rejection I realized that I had to find a way not to accept no as an answer.

I needed a good place to think, where I could clear my mind and start the process anew. One of my releases has always been working out. Totally stressed, I went to the gym and ran on the treadmill trying to conjure up a solution. The drone of the motor and the belt got my brain working. I had to alter the perception and convince people of the merit of our transaction. I really believed I was a victim of bad timing and was right about what we were undertaking. I realized that it's so easy to say no especially when someone just doesn't want to be open minded.

I also came to the realization that a no could not be turned into an immediate yes, but perhaps it could be upgraded into a maybe. From there, it would not be a big leap to a yes. I had to pry open the door in some way and drive a wedge in there while I made my pitch. By turning my sales presentation into a two-tier step from simply "talking the deal," I was consciously quantifying the task.

My immediate goal in the next conversation was to convince the no responses to reconsider as maybe considerations.

On my next call, I tried this approach:

"Hi, Jack, it's me, Jeff. I was wondering if you've had a chance to review the information I sent you regarding the Hampton development."

"I looked at it. It really isn't for me." (I assumed he never looked at the package.)

"Jack, I appreciate you taking the time to read the materials. May I ask you just one question?"

"Sure, go ahead."

"My partner and I have all the money to our name down on contract deposits on this transaction. If I don't close it, I can go find a job. Either I am insane to take the risk to try to do this deal, or I really have something that makes a lot of sense. If it does make sense, then at the end of the day there is a lot of money to be made for our partners and us. I know that the change in the tax laws has created the perception that real estate is not where you should invest right now.

"Call me a contrarian, but I know this is a great opportunity. Either way, would you give me fifteen minutes of your time so I can tell you what I see? At the end of our chat if what I have to say is of no interest, I will say fine and walk away. At the very least, you will be more informed. Maybe you will be surprised, and you will see the value in the transaction."

I had subtly but materially transformed the intent of our conversation from his point of view.

Jack really could not say no to giving me fifteen minutes, and I quickly scheduled a meeting.

 Rule 14   Always get in front of the person you are trying to sell. Look them in the eyes and take control.

After my pitch in person, Jack saw my conviction and passion and agreed with the merits of my assumptions. He was willing to continue listening and actually to consider the deal. I had moved Jack from no to maybe. He told me that he and his brother might possibly invest $100,000 each in the transaction.

This was a revelation and a small victory. More than that, it gave me the confidence to approach others in the same fashion.

The soft no occurs when a good salesman gets a negative response but detects a slight opening—an opening that could potentially lead to a maybe. It takes practice and good judgment to note the subtleties. Each situation is discrete, and each situation may require a modification in your language and in the intensity of your pitch. It depends on the individual and on your perception of that individual. If a potential customer said to me, "I have absolutely no interest in real estate" or whatever it is I'm working on, and it's something he just doesn't want to do, then I would say, "That's fine. Thank you for being candid." Then I might casually ask, "So what is it that you do? Are you currently investing? What are the areas that you do have interest in? Do you invest in the market? Do you look at pipe transactions?" A pipe transaction stands for a Private Investment in Public Entity. (I wouldn't ask all these questions at once, of course; I'd try to discern which one might elicit a response that gets the person to open up.)

I might try to flatter the person in a low-key way. I could say, "You're obviously good at what you do and successful, so I'm sure you invest your savings in some kind of financial instrument; what areas are you interested in? Right now, I'm talking to you about my core business, but there are other things that I do. And I'm interested in learning, because you never know what I'll see in the marketplace that might be compelling to you. Or, I may know somebody else who can help you achieve some of your goals."

In the first deal we were doing, I had to transform every no into a maybe, and I knew the most effective way to do this was to get in front of every potential investor.

The approach I used with Jack was very effective. Virtually every person I spoke with gave me an audience. The maybes started to turn into yeses, and we were getting closer to raising the necessary capital.

Each week would end like a boxing round. I would head off to my corner exhausted; but, after the weekend was over, I was ready to recharge and start the battle all over again Monday morning. I still approached the phone with tremendous trepidation, but the doors were beginning to budge.

The pressure was on, however. We were only three weeks away from closing on the real estate and we were still $500,000 short. Jack and his brother were a potential $200,000, but by now they had stopped returning my phone calls. Had maybe reverted to no? One more time, I thought. I called Jack's secretary, but she told me that he was unavailable and would call back.

Annoyed, I hung up the phone and looked at Marc.

"Let's go," I said.

"Where are we going?" he wondered.

"We're going to see Jack. I'm tired of not getting my calls returned."

Jack was in the messenger business. His office was in a walk-up building on Third Avenue. Marc and I trudged up the stairs to his office. I was so nervous that sweat was beading on my forehead. I almost couldn't believe I was about to just barge in on this guy. I entered the reception area, opened the door, walked past his secretary, and opened the door to Jack's office. He was on the phone deep in conversation staring down at the floor. He looked up at me and motioned with his hand one second. I stood in front of his desk with my arms crossed. A minute later, he hung up the phone and I immediately lunged.

"Jack, I am tired of your jerking me around," I blurted. "I've called you several times and you haven't had the decency to call me back. My life is committed to this deal, and I'm going to make it work."

I reiterated all the parameters of the transaction again. My enthusiasm was palpable and hopefully contagious. I raced to the finish, and I looked at Jack and delivered my closing argument.

"I am going to succeed with these properties. And I really want you and your brother to be part of this success," I concluded.

"Okay," he said.

The turning point. I couldn't believe this move worked.

Jack pulled out his checkbook and called his brother. We were $200,000 closer. I raised the remaining amount of money using a similar approach on two other occasions.

I don't necessarily recommend that you waltz past the secretaries of recalcitrant sales prospects the way that I did as a matter of standard procedure. I assume you will use more conventional means to schedule appointments. At that time, I was young, naïve, and desperate. Desperate times called for desperate measures. But when I finally did meet with Jack, I was able to deploy all of my sales weapons.

Will this kind of aggressive behavior work for everyone? For you? I can't answer that. Many people will probably be put off by this approach—and yes, the guy could have called security and had me thrown out of his office. I could make the argument that if Bernstein and Woodward thought twice about disturbing a potential source's dinner at his home during Watergate, President Nixon might have served out his second term and the full story might never have been told. When you think about it, those reporters were probably more brazen in their behavior than your typical telemarketer. I did what I needed to do given the time and the situation. That's the lesson to be learned here.

When you are finally face-to-face with the potential customer, you want to convey integrity, strength, intelligence, and confidence. That sounds like a lot to digest, but it isn't. All those characteristics emanate from your eyes and the way you conduct yourself. Think about the things that you say while you're looking someone in the eyes. I feel that whomever I speak to, I've got their rapt attention. If I don't have it, I'll shift; I'll move somewhere else. I can usually tell if I don't have somebody. And I'll react. It's often visceral, or a sixth sense. It has taken some time to develop this skill. But I know that when I speak to someone, and I'm focused on whatever it might be, I control the conversation. I'm temperate, but I turn the dial up or down as necessary. I'll be knowledgeable but not arrogant. I'll be strong but not overpowering. I'll exude confidence but also show a humble side. And while I'll frame my deal in the best possible light, I will be totally up front and honest.

How can you tell when your subject is losing interest? There are a lot of variables, a lot of moving parts. You have to evaluate the person's level of understanding and interest. Is he or she smart enough to get what I'm talking about? Or am I talking to him or her and it's far above the person's comprehension. How detailed are you going to get? I like specifics, but others don't. Normally, the more intelligent people ask the more detailed questions.

You must constantly evaluate your audience and understand their capacity or lack of capacity for understanding and interest. Some very bright people just won't have an interest in things that you might have an interest in. And you've got to read the results. I often see it in their eyes. Some people don't have the desire to look under the hood. So I know that I can't go into detail with them. These people are interested only in asking two questions: What's the bottom line, and what's my risk? I actually enjoy it more, however, when someone says, "Explain it to me, how does it work?" You've got to read your customers, know when you're losing them, and know how to react to them when you do.

This is crucial to becoming a "likeable" person. Being likeable is mandatory because nearly every study shows that people like to buy products and services from people they like. In an election campaign, people vote for the candidate they *like* (even when they swear up and down that they're focusing on the issues). The candidates are selling ideas and policies, certainly; but more important, they're selling themselves. People don't buy the candidate's issues; they buy the candidate's likeability quotient. That's why political campaigns spend so much money on focus groups. It's very nearly the same in business.

In the early stages of your career, your success has more to do with talent, skill, and hard work. As you advance, your results are more tied to how well you get along with people. Also, once you're typed as being "difficult" (or, not that likeable), it is a personality trait that follows you far more than you think. It's a hard label to shake. You might not even know that you didn't get a job or close a deal because someone didn't like you.

It's better to be liked than disliked. It's an obvious point. If you're likeable, more opportunities will come your way. People will want to introduce you, help you find new contacts, and aid you in your quest to develop new business.

BE BOLD BUT POLITE, PERSISTENT BUT PATIENT

A lesson to be learned is that people invest in people. Jack probably was shocked that I did what I did to get him to go in on our deal. I eventually convinced him, however, that I was a winner. I discovered that being brazen and forceful in a polite way made me appear incredibly determined, and Jack was betting that my determination would get positive results.

Recently, when my partner and I rehashed this experience with Jack, Marc commented that most people couldn't do what I did. They didn't have the talent and fortitude to just walk into someone's office and all but demand that they make a decision. But I disagreed. Most people absolutely could do what I did. They just choose not to. You have to have the guts to ask.

In this case, I was driven by desperation. You need not wait until this point. It's basic assertiveness training. Granted, I might have been a little headstrong, but I felt it was better to err on the side of aggression than timidity. What did I have to lose? The next time you're confronted with a situation where you're contemplating taking bold action, ask yourself, "What's my downside?" If your worst-case scenario is rejection, you have no excuse not to ask.

One of my friends, David Gensler, was in a similar situation— albeit further along in his career—when he had a specific situation where he was being rejected for no apparently logical reason. David, whose specialty is in managing pension plans, was trying to get a potential client to shift millions of dollars of business to his firm. He had been incessantly pitching his plan, but he finally hit a wall. He had done a lot of homework, made a number of sales calls, and wasn't getting anywhere. When he sought my advice, I could see he was clearly frustrated. He was going out to see this guy again, and he was basically getting shut down. He decided his plan of attack should be full force. He said, "I'll tell them you should be using me because I can do this, I can do that . . ." And he was sitting there, and he was really worked up, and I said to him, "You're doing totally the wrong thing."

He looked at me and said, "Well, they're not being responsive."

I asked, "Why?"

He didn't answer. I said, "You don't even know why they're not hiring you. So before you go and jump at them, ask the question. You did everything they asked you to do, and they've decided to stay where they are. *Why?* What is their perception of the benefit of staying where they are?" David's plan was to go back to the customer and reiterate why his company should be their choice, essentially repeating his standard sales pitch. Why would you want to repeat what hadn't worked?

Let's analyze what was really going on here: David had been focused on what he and his firm does best—managing assets, tracking the money flow, worrying about the specific benefits to his clients, how the participants have access to their funds. These are the types of questions and methodologies that he typically must explain throughout his whole presentation. But the simple question—and important issue—of the process of switching from one pension-fund manager to another didn't even come up. It's not something that he zeroed in on because, like most people in his position, he was too preoccupied with the obvious—selling hard. Everybody says, "We can do it better." At the end of the day, they liked David, but they hesitated when they thought about the difficulty of changing. Their excuse was wafer thin. "We have all these employees, we've got to fill out forms, and have them sign papers. It's a distraction. We're too busy; we're running a company."

I went on, telling David that he had to emphasize that "well, you don't do anything. I do all the paper work. There's no hassle. I take care of everything. It's seamless." That should evoke a different response.

That's what ultimately happened, and he wound up closing the deal. In fact, the client was relieved. He was surprised to hear that David's firm would take care of all the logistics, all the bureaucratic red tape.

The client's perception had been wrong. It wasn't on the table as an issue, but when David approached it and asked, "What is your perception? What do you see? Why would you want to stay where you are if I can really demonstrate that I can do a lot better things for your employees? What is your reservation?" Now he knew what he had to attack. He handled it the right way by understanding the real issue. When someone says no, try to understand *why* it's no.

You have to approach each day as an opportunity, and you have to maintain a positive attitude despite adversity. Basically, this is what I did when I was faced with the challenge of closing that first deal. I transformed the fear of failure into a motivating force. You have to love the challenge of what you do, especially if it's convincing a client to buy your goods or services. You've got to *believe* in what you're selling. If you don't, there's almost no chance you will get a difficult prospect to buy from you. Accept the fact that everyone who is good at what he does has suffered a crushing rejection at one time or another—usually more than once. Have the mind-set that the person who told you no thinks he's rejecting you (or your product or service), but you're going to go back until you get what you want. This takes a combination of patience and persistence, and everyone can develop these two traits if he or she just commits to doing it.

7

The Art of the Sale

One of the most telling moments in the art of selling comes from fiction. In David Mamet's 1992 film *Glengarry Glen Ross* about a group of desperate real estate agents, Al Pacino plays an ultraslick salesman named Ricky Roma. In a key scene, Roma meets a guy in a bar and buys him a drink. The guy is obviously a little shy, but he's lonely, and after some small talk, Roma begins asking him about his life, his aspirations, and so on. This goes on for some time. Roma nods a lot and buys the man a couple more rounds. When they are both relaxed, he casually pulls out a brochure, spreads it on the table, and begins explaining a piece of property. You may or may not be interested, he says with brilliant subtlety, shrugging his shoulders just so, almost as if he didn't care. Though Mamet spares the viewer any further details, by the end of the evening, Roma has made a sale. But the next day, the buyer unexpectedly backs out of the purchase, and when Roma calls to find out why, he learns that his wife was the one who didn't approve. It's never clear whether this excuse is valid or not but no amount of Roma's cajoling can convince him to change his mind.

You can learn a lot from this scene, even though it ultimately turns quickly and dramatically from a yes to a no. Pacino's character studies his prospect, makes the appropriate eye contact, lets him talk, listens carefully, takes plenty of time to learn what he's about, and never pressures him. The scene makes an impact because it reveals a psychology behind the pitch, the idea that the prospect will have to like and trust the man who is selling him; and that, ultimately, perception of what he's buying plays a large part. He is buying a piece of paradise, though his wife supposedly disabuses him of this notion.

The ultimate lesson is that there is no sale unless you know the buyers.

A sale occurs when the potential buyer perceives a need or else has a want for the product. Did the guy in the movie need the land that Ricky Roma was selling? Probably not. Sales are often more about desire than necessity. Many times price is the key variable. Who can resist a bargain? Sometimes the buyer thinks the purchase is a great deal when, in fact, the sale is a deception. Integrity of the sale separates those who are in business now and those who stay in business tomorrow. It is important to understand the parameters of the sale, both good and bad.

It's important to understand that we either are being sold or are selling. That is simply the way of the world. If you are pure salesman, your product could be widgets or jet fighters. Some of us may have lofty titles or advanced degrees from prominent universities; but, at the end of the day, we are all still salesmen. Even purists like research scientists have to sell their ideas, apply for grants, and convince the world that their theories have validity. Lawyers sell their knowledge and their ability to apply it to win cases or settlements. Doctors sell their knowledge of medicine and their ability to cure. Think of any profession, and, on some level, a sale is always in motion.

The top sales personnel obviously are somewhat rare and deserve large compensation packages. They are the business generators, the rainmakers. And because they bring in a company's revenues, they are paid very well. Few would dispute their paychecks, especially those who thrive on commissions, overrides, and pieces of deals. I'm not sure whether great salesmen are made or born; it's not an issue worth much debate in my view. Certainly anyone not directly related to sales can improve the networking tools he or she needs to succeed.

The most successful salesmen are the ones who sell a good product and have long-term aspirations. They are thinking about keeping customers for life, rather than for a single sale. They want to do business with their clients in such a way that the clients will continue to want to do business with them. This means the client has to perceive value in every transaction. Those who sell anything regardless of merit just to make a quick dollar inevitably will fail at some point.

Unfortunately, there are many businesses that run their operations predicated solely on making a sale today and not caring about tomorrow. We have all been on the receiving end of some unscrupulous purveyor of goods or services. Who hasn't, at some point, felt like he has been taken advantage of? We merely cut our losses and move on.

If you live in a metropolitan market like New York, Miami, or Los Angeles, you may have noticed the abundance of the small electronics, camera, and film stores that saturate areas with high pedestrian traffic, often tourists. I knew someone, a casual acquaintance, who had a part-time job working in such a store in New York City. The particular store he worked for always had a sale going on.

"Lost our lease, everything has to go." Sound familiar? Of course, the sign is fallacious and merely implies that the items in the store are bargains because the store is going out of business.

"Fifty percent off all merchandise." Another ridiculous notion, since the buyer never has a chance to learn what the suggested retail price is. So it's half off some inflated figure, which you can never really learn. The consumer assumes he's getting a good deal, but he's being deceived. These stores lure in the naïve and take advantage of them.

This type of sales tactic preys on a consumer's greed and ignorance. And at one point, I debated whether to discuss this in the book, but I'm continually surprised by how easily people are taken in.

It is easy for reasonably intelligent people to be fooled by sophisticated approaches.

The bait-and-switch sales tactic is hardly complicated, but it is one of the most time-honored and unscrupulous forms of doing business. Unfortunately, it's still commonly practiced today. Generally, there's a sign in the storefront window advertising very low prices on certain goods. Often, these products are last year's models, currently crowding the store's inventory. (There's a reason these products didn't sell last year—they weren't attractive, either in price or usefulness.) The markups in the retail electronic business, generally, are very thin. The discount items in the window are usually priced a little above what the staff would call the "C-Line"—store code for the cost to the store. Take, for example, a Kodak Instamatic camera without a flash that had a sale price of $29.95. The wholesale cost to the store was $26.00, so $3.95 wasn't much of a profit. On a daily basis, at least a few people would come into the store and request the Kodak camera.

The salesman would take the customer over to the counter where the camera was showcased. The conversation typically went something like this.

"Would you like the camera, sir?" asked the salesman.

"Okay, I'll take it."

"Let me get your name for the guarantee."

The salesman would pull out the store sales pad and start to fill in the information. After the sale was completed, the salesman would then ask, "By the way sir, did you know that we are having a special today on the deluxe Continental Instant camera? This camera has a built-in flash, and it's regularly $79.95, but it's on sale today only for $49.95."

The salesman takes the Continental camera out of the showcase and puts it on the counter. The customer picks up the camera, looks at it, and says, "Gee, it looks nice, but I really didn't want to spend that much."

The salesman explains that this model is far superior to the Kodak because it has a Fosterized Duraplastic lens (there are no such words as "Fosterized" and "Duraplastic"), which makes the pictures five times sharper than the Kodak's (also not true). He emphasizes the built-in flash by convincing the customer that he can save $2.90 a picture for the flash bars.

"This camera is worth the additional money without a question," the salesman says. "You really should take advantage of this great deal."

"Is it really that big of a difference?"

"It's regularly $79.95—that should tell you something."

"I don't know."

The customer hesitates and then decides to buy the Kodak.

But then the salesman says that he'll take an additional $5 off the price (he has plenty of profit margin, he could even take another $5 off if he has to). He eventually makes the sale. With a touch of hubris, he bids good-bye by reminding the customer to "send me your friends when they need something."

This practice of lowering the price to push the customer over the edge is called dropping line. I'm not sure whether it refers to letting out a trolling line and hoping to hook a fish, but it certainly seems that way in retrospect.

My friend who worked in the electronics store invited me to spend a couple of afternoons watching him and the others sell. It was an amazing show at times, as unsuspecting customers continually bought high-markup items that were inferior products. The ethics involved in this story reflect a very low level of character. A customer buys an off-brand for $45 that cost the store only $12. The salesman made a triple markup as opposed to selling a far more legitimate $26 item for $30.

There were other scams. Sometimes they would sell a portable radio/cassette player for cost. When ringing up the sale, they would ask the customer if he wanted to buy the accessories kit. The kit consisted of the electric cord, earphone, and batteries ($29.95). The customer almost always bought it. It was all part of the unit, but the store simply removed it and sold it separately.

Watching these tactics made me better at what I do now. First, it showed by example how *not* to develop long-term relationships with customers. These salesmen knew that once a customer figured out what really happened, they were doing one-shot deals. Only truly ignorant ones would keep coming back. Second, the daily contact with buyers illustrated how important it was to get as close as possible to whomever you were trying to sell.

Retailers have certain advantages, one of the most important being that the customer is in their presence. It instilled in me the critical nature of a face-to-face meeting with any prospect.

BEWARE OF A COMMON FAULT: TRYING TOO HARD

Despite all your success, one of the worst positions a salesperson can find himself in is one where he is overselling the customer. It's a subtle line that is easily crossed, and nothing can scotch a deal faster. When a prospective customer—even a fairly receptive one—sees that someone is trying too hard, it immediately creates a negative impression. At the very least it begs the question, "Is the salesman desperate?"

Overselling is a sales technique generally used by inexperienced or uninformed salespeople. Recently, I was invited to a presentation made by a private investment fund, where a stockbroker acquaintance of my firm has an affiliation. The stockbroker was very aggressive in his sales pitch. He told me that his clients were jumping at the opportunity to invest in this fund.

This man's credibility has always been somewhat suspect to me, mainly because he always sells using superlatives. Every instrument he wields is "the best," a "can't miss," and the "best opportunity you'll see in the next year." His analytical skills are minimal. He generally doesn't even understand the financials of the company he is pitching. Regardless, I always hear him out because there are possibilities. Besides, you never know whom you will meet at one of his open pitches.

I arrived at the event and was stunned to see that only ten people were there. We had been in a down-market cycle, but ten people in attendance is an embarrassment nonetheless. I couldn't believe this stockbroker told me his clients were jumping at the opportunity to participate in the fund. The presenter was engaging and bright but spoke far too long. After forty-five minutes, his audience had dwindled to five. I decided to leave as well. My stockbroker friend stopped me at the elevator.

"So what did you think, Jeff?"

"It was interesting."

"My clients are going crazy for this," he said. "I am going to raise $200 million dollars for this fund."

I looked at him in disbelief. This guy obviously doesn't see himself as others do. Imagine that few people showed up for the event, and he is blissfully unaware of the disappointing turnout. The statement indicated that he is out of touch with reality. Only a month earlier, I saw him at the health club, and he was bemoaning how poorly the equities markets were faring. He even speculated that he might leave the brokerage business to go into my business. He had a client with $5 million to invest in real estate, he said; but if this was true, I would have heard about it.

 Rule 15

After you pry it open, always try to keep the door ajar. When you see the opening, that's when you can attack.

Most salespeople disregard certain prospects as impossible to sell, but with some exceptions, I never have. I was convinced of this when I did my first deal, and I converted numerous clients who seemed unreceptive and immovable.

Here are some of the most important things to remember when your client is seated across the table:

- ➤ Always make direct eye contact. The worst thing you can do is to speak to someone looking down at the floor or in another direction. If you have a tendency to do this (and you'd be surprised how often people do it), begin correcting it. Concentrate. Look deep into those pupils. If you don't, the impression you will leave is either that you have no confidence or you're less than honest.
- ➤ Avoid the dreaded monotone; you will put your prospect to sleep. Once a colleague told me that he was about to buy a mattress from a salesman at Sleepy's. The salesman was nice enough, but he was so soft-spoken and dull that he decided not to buy the bed. It became a joke—the salesman at Sleepy's was asleep. Use voice inflection.
- ➤ Enthusiasm expresses belief in the product. If you are not excited about what you are selling, chances are that you are not going to excite the prospect and make the sale.

➤ Know your product well. Create a template that explains the important characteristics of the product without overwhelming the person with too much detail (unless he or she asks).

➤ Don't talk too much. Listen and observe. Customer responses and reactions are tremendously important. If your pitch isn't working and the prospect is shutting down, stop selling. Once I see one of my prospects losing interest—usually shown by fidgeting or wandering eyes—I immediately abbreviate my pitch and ask the prospect about his business. My strategy is to wake him up. Everyone loves to talk about himself. His eyes wake up, and he starts to explain the details of his business. He is effectively starting to sell me. Why did I do this? My gut reaction told me I wasn't going to make the sale. I'd look for new synergies for a future sale.

➤ There is always tomorrow. It is impossible to close everyone all the time. Plant the seeds, build the resources, and enter the individual in your database as a resource for whatever his or her expertise is. This strategy facilitates building your resources and potentially sharing them with others.

➤ Respond to your visceral sense—your gut reaction typically is correct. Aside from presenting well, you must make accurate judgments about the prospect and modify your approach on the fly. Some people seem totally unreceptive to any kind of pitch. The "reverse-reversal" is a tool that enables you to approach the unapproachable. If you engage the customers directly, you will capture a certain percentage of the market merely because it is a game of numbers.

One of my friends works on Wall Street and is a brilliant salesman. Phil specializes in medical products and related technology companies. I was in his office listening to him on the phone. He was selling a prospective client on a new venture. Based on the depth of questions Phil was answering, I could tell that the person on the other end of the line was well versed in Phil's area of expertise. The sales pitch went on for five minutes or so, and Phil was relentless. He was going full speed ahead, and the prospect continued to repel the assault. Phil's potential client said he would think about the opportunity. Phil didn't make the sale.

Later that day I asked him about how he thought the conversation had gone. Phil told me that it is difficult to get anybody to focus on this particular medical company. At the time, the apathy for the market was at its height and people were not interested in investing in Phil's medical company.

"Phil, you might want to try an approach I call the reverse-reversal," I said.

"What is that?" he asked.

"Well it's sort of selling someone from the side," I said. "It's so subtle that they really don't know that you are selling them."

"Go on."

"Do you really think this medical company is a great buy?"

"Jeff, it's trading at an all-time low and their financial results have never been better. It is just a casualty of a bear market. In the long term, I firmly believe it will be recognized for the value that it is, and the price will rise accordingly."

I understood what he meant. In a down market, investors just shut down regardless of an investment's merit. When he called the prospect, Phil felt that he had already made his decision and that decision was a firm no. But it wasn't necessarily true. He engaged in a conversation with him regardless. "He was predisposed prior to your talk," I said. "His expertise in his field is exactly where your opportunity to capture his interest lies." I suggested, "Next time, why don't you call him and say, 'Bob, I was

wondering if you would do me a favor. I am seriously considering increasing my position in ABC medical products company. I
have been following the company for a while, and I'm intimately
familiar with their products and their position in the market.
Because of your knowledge of this industry, and the respect I
have for your opinion, would you mind if I sent you some information on this company? I would really appreciate if you would
take a look at it and tell me what you think.' He can't say no. He
believes your decision is contingent upon his insight."

Phil's eyes lit up. He got it.

Think about the difference between the two approaches. The
prospect on the direct sale approach was defensive; he knew he
was being pitched; and he was predisposed to say no before Phil
opened his mouth. With the reverse-reversal approach you are
asking the prospect for his opinion. You are inflating his ego,
and he will look at the opportunity objectively because he thinks
it is for you and not for him. He may ultimately have an interest
in it. If your analysis is correct, and he reviews the materials and
concludes that he is favorably disposed to the company, you will
affirm your skills in picking a stock. He will tell you to increase
your position and probably will be inclined to buy the stock for
himself.

8

The Database

It's What You Know About Who You Know

Here is a scenario I'm certain you'll recognize. You're at a business cocktail party where there must be a hundred or so strangers and a few of your colleagues. You spend ten minutes catching up on company gossip with your coworkers, and then you stroll to the bar. While waiting for a drink, you start a conversation with the person standing next to you. The discussion is engaging; you have a few things in common, perhaps even a customer or a contact. Twenty minutes later, when both of you realize it's time to work the room, you exchange business cards and suggest getting together at some future time. When you return to your office, you put the business card in your desk drawer or in a file box.

Six months later, during your semi-annual office cleanup and update, you discover the card and have absolutely no idea who this person is. So, how many times have you done this? If you are like most people, it has probably happened more than once. Once, as a guest speaker at a business luncheon, I began by asking the audience if they'd had this experience. Nearly every hand went up. I wasn't surprised. Most of us go to business cocktail parties to meet people and to create future potential opportunities. Yet once the evening ends, we don't have the slightest recollection of whom we met and what they do.

What good is making a contact if you never follow up?

If there is no system to capture the information about the various people you meet, you will seriously limit yourself in developing potential resources. If you have fallen into this behavior pattern, you need to make a greater effort to become organized. If you don't, you're probably better off working late at the office. Understand how to quantify and classify your contact information, and you'll see a major difference in your business.

GERRY AND HIS SIX ROLODEXES

Early in my career I was introduced to a real estate broker, Gerry Rosenblum. Rosenblum was a senior partner in his firm and well known to the real estate community. Often Rosenblum's name was listed as the representing broker on the tombstone ads in the newspapers, typically announcements for large transactions. Reporters quoted him in their stories about the real estate market. He was a bona fide authority in his field.

A mutual friend facilitated an introduction for me to Rosenblum in his office. Our meeting was short, but it left an indelible impression on me. We chatted for about a half hour, and Gerry walked me through some of his more successful transactions.

Toward the end of the meeting, Rosenblum swiveled his chair around and proudly pointed to six Rolodexes on the credenza behind him.

"You see these Rolodexes?" he said. "There are five thousand contacts in there. I know everybody. In fact, there isn't a CEO of a major corporation I can't call on a deal. That's why I get the opportunities I do."

Six full Rolodexes, five thousand contacts. That certainly is a lot of people to know. I was suitably impressed. After the meeting, I thought about Rosenblum and his six Rolodexes. Did he really actively know who all those people were? Years ago when I used a Rolodex, I had trouble keeping track of the people in it. One day my secretary took it upon herself to revamp my Rolodex. I couldn't find someone I routinely called. It was a cumbersome system. I needed something better.

Finger-stained Rolodexes should reside next to the old type-writer in the storage room. It amazes me how many people still use such an outmoded method. In fact, my own partner has one. I am constantly urging him to join the twenty-first century and input his contacts onto a database in his computer. He won't do it. He's not a technophobe (he uses a computer all the time). Some people are just resistant to change or balk because it seems like too much work.

There is no question that a properly maintained contact data-base will allow you to be a more productive and effective net-worker. This is a change you need to make if you want your contact list to be useful.

Existing electronic tools can make you more efficient and will provide the ability to transport your information anywhere.

Palm Pilots, Blackberrys, Compaq Ipaqs, and other personal digital assistants (or PDAs, as they're commonly called) have transformed the way data is stored and retrieved. Thanks to the boom in wireless communication, you can be in instant commu-nication with people in your business arc (and even get real-time stock quotes) from virtually any location on the planet. I don't go anywhere without my PDA. I receive and send e-mails at the airport, in cabs, and at home. I can work anywhere, and I'm al-ways accessible. Airports have finally recognized the need for wireless high-speed connections, and several in the United States have installed them to accommodate business travelers while they wait for flights.

The foundation to everything I do is built into my database.

It is constantly in flux, updated almost daily. The database software that I use is Goldmine. (Indeed, the creators of this software could not have thought of a more appropriate name.) There are several other programs that are equally as good. The information you input includes what would normally be in a Rolodex, but it's more comprehensive, easier to alter. The basic fields include the contact's name, title, reference, and phone number, and perhaps most important, notes. This is standard on competitive software. Where the programs principally differ is in their categorization of data and communication functions.

For instance, you can customize all of your contacts by industry. Many of my searches begin here. If I were looking for an institutional investor who has an interest in technology, I would send an e-mail to attorneys who specialize in securities and investment bankers.

PHONE, E-MAIL, OR SNAIL MAIL

I cannot emphasize how important e-mail has become in the business world. In the last five years it has become an indispensable communications tool. Why? It is faster, more reliable, and more efficient than a letter, but it is still somewhat slower and more complex than using a phone.

I still prefer the phone in many instances, and so do many other businessmen. On the phone, you can detect nuances in a person's responses that you cannot in an e-mail. If you're discussing a deal, the dead silences, the voice raising, the enthusiasm or skepticism all leaks through. You can't have a conference call on e-mail.

E-mail is one voice at a time, direct. There's no subtlety in e-mail, and occasionally you see attempts at irony, humor, and sarcasm that are accidentally misinterpeted.

But e-mail itself is a wonderful tool because it leaves a linear, easy-to-follow paper trail of whatever project you're working on. It's easy to see where anyone stands in the course of a discussion. The only negative is the perception of privacy and security. Both of these are huge issues that have been addressed by the technology industry, but they haven't yet been solved. (So far, it's easier to invade one's privacy and steal information from a computer than raid his mailbox.) An endearing trait of e-mail is that it involves a synchronous communication. It eliminates phone tag. You respond at your convenience. Your formatting does not need to be "business letter perfect." (Though you should pay attention to syntax and grammar, especially if you're e-mailing someone you don't know well.)

Here are some of the ways you can communicate using your database:

Under the "lookup" icon there are filters that allow me to send e-mails to virtually any category I choose. I can e-mail only real estate attorneys or only people who live in New York. I can create a customized list by using area codes, or individuals whose first name is Jack or any field that caters to my interest.

The search function can be usefully applied to the notes section for each contact. I am religious about putting the following in notes: how I met the contact, through whom, companies they may be affiliated with, and a description of their individual skill sets. Being able to search these references when needed further enhances my system. A recent example illustrates how valuable my accumulated data has become. At the time of this writing, I am working on an investment opportunity in China. I went to the "look up" section and entered the word "China." The software searched my entire database and found twenty-three contacts that have the word "China" in my notes section. These individuals who have an interest or affiliation are now one phone call (or e-mail) away.

An added feature is that the software can make the e-mail appear to be more personal than it really is. The recipient of the e-mail doesn't see hundreds of names above the e-mail, as with many common mass e-mailings. Most people delete e-mails that have been received by a large list of recipients because they look like spam. Pay attention to the vagaries of electronic etiquette. I would suggest that you limit your mass mailings for instances when it really matters, simply because we're being inundated with quasi-junk e-mail every day. Your credibility is inversely proportional to the frivolousness of your use of this technology. When I receive dozens of jokes and announcements from someone, it lowers the value of their substantive communiqués. Think before you send a mass e-mail. Too many frivolous ones will devalue your message when you have something substantive to say.

There are other features I'm sure Goldmine mavens have discovered that I don't even know about. But just the program's basic structure alone has been enough to make me a more effective businessman.

> ### Rule 16
>
> It is who you know. But more important is *what* you know about *who* you know.

Here is an example of how I put my database to work. I decided to sponsor a luncheon with a friend who is a senior executive of a firm called U.S. Trust. The theme of the lunch was Entrepreneurs in Transition. I sent the following e-mail to everyone in my database.

```
From: jeffm@mercurycap.com
To: [Contact list]
Subject: Entrepreneur Luncheon
```

```
Dear _____:
Re: Entrepreneurs in Transition
March 7th or 18th
```

```
    On Thursday, March 7 and Monday, March 18, Kary
Presten of U.S. Trust and I are cohosting a luncheon,
which is part of an ongoing series to address the grow-
ing number of business owners and corporate execu-
tives who have exited their businesses and who are
looking for new opportunities. This luncheon series
will provide a unique forum for this fortunate subset
of society to openly discuss their ideas and concerns
about their future with similarly situated people. Due
to the overwhelming interest in our topic, we have
decided to have the luncheon on two separate dates to
accommodate all those who would like to participate.
The luncheon will be held at U.S. Trust, located at
114 W. 47 St. (between 6th and 7th Ave.) beginning at
noon.
    Please RSVP to Kary Presten (212) 555-3939 or kpreston@
ustrust.com and please include your name, address,
telephone number, e-mail and industry that you are in-
volved in so we can include you in this unique event.
```

```
    Best regards, Jeffrey
```

I received more than 150 responses, and we filled both lun-
cheons. (We had a waiting list of those who want to attend a future event.) The age of the participants ranged from twenty-five
to seventy-five. The gamut of industries represented went from
the old guard bricks-and-mortars guys to the Internet guys who
were fortunate enough to cash out before the crash. The list of

attendees and industries represented included telecommunications, pharmaceutical, and food company executives; retail and finance entrepreneurs; and media and TV executives; in short, a grab bag of talented professionals with accomplished careers. One of my clients, a psychiatrist, e-mailed me and said he wished he were an entrepreneur in transition. He did have a good friend who sold his medical device company, however. Today, the friend only invests and devotes free time to promoting his charities. He suggested I call him. I did, and he attended. He turned out to be a terrific guy and an excellent resource. (Recently, his brother met with me to suggest doing joint venture real estate transactions.)

The agenda included questions such as, "Is life after exiting your business what you expected? What are your unmet goals? How do you define success? What is your wish list? How can the group help?" It ended with a session that suggested what steps should be taken.

The part of the program that asked, "What is your wish list?" was very revealing. Most of the participants said that they wanted to get back out there and serve on corporate or charitable boards, and in some cases, run a new business. After the event, I met with most of the participants individually. I learned more specifically their areas of expertise and what they wanted to do.

Rule 17 Follow up—and continue to follow up—after the event.

What happens after such an event? How do you maximize its value? You should follow up with all the contacts you made at the event. Think beyond the cocktail party. Here is a brief summary of my activity that occurred after this particular meeting:

Arnold (*Mergers and Acquisitions*): I introduced him to an investment banking firm, where I'm a member of the advisory board. He has since joined the board of one of the companies the firm represents.

David (*Technology*): I introduced him to another friend who sold his company in a similar industry. They have had multiple meetings and are pursuing opportunities together.

Gary (*Real Estate*): I introduced him to a company that was involved in an area that interested Gary. That company is now negotiating with him to be involved in some kind of advisory capacity.

Cliff (*Technology*): After several introductions, Cliff landed a CEO position for a company funded by a large venture capital firm.

Robert (*Consumer Products*): Perhaps the wealthiest participant at the luncheon, Robert said, "Money isn't the issue anymore. Let's face it. If any of us had another $10 million, would it really change our lives?" Success comes in different forms for different people. (Yes, his comment startled some of the less well-heeled participants.)

Michael (*Telecommunications*): An expert on telecom transactions, Michael is assisting me with introductions to resources in the industry. Currently, I am representing a video-conferencing company.

Bill (*Apparel*): Bill is anxious to run a new company. I introduced him to at least a dozen different contacts. He just led me to a new client.

In February 2003, I held this event again with different hosts. This time John Oden from Alliance Capital Management and Robert Israel who mediates Young Presidents Organization members-in-transition forums were my partners.

> Create platforms, and you will create opportunities. A platform is anything where you are the impresario. It can be a luncheon, an entrepreneur-in-transition event, a private dinner for clients, a charity event that you create and/or host.

I e-mailed a similar invitation through my database. This time I had 350 responses, more than double the first time I did it. We held two events, a breakfast and a lunch, and each had thirty-five attendees. Again, the participants were very successful business people in multiple industries. This time we featured entrepreneurs who sold their businesses at the top and bought them back at a discounted price. One of the panelists literally sold his company for $70 million and bought it back from the acquirer for only $2 million. Surprisingly, this type of outcome isn't rare in today's volatile world of commerce. Quaker Oats bought Snapple for $1.7 billion, mismanaged the brand, and then sold it to Triarc for $300 million, a spectacular loss. There are a number of business people who make a living at corporate garage sales.

PHILANTHROPY GROWS OUT OF NETWORKING, TOO

I serve on a board with a man named Jerry Menkin. Jerry owns a highly regarded jewelry business in New York. Recently my wife lost a diamond chip in a bracelet. I asked Jerry if he could replace the chip. He said it would cost $80, but he didn't want to charge me. Instead, he had a particular charity that he was very involved with. Would I write a check directly to the charity? What a nice idea. Of course.

Then the lights went on. Why not extend the goodwill a bit further? I checked with Jerry, and then I drafted the following e-mail that I would send to my entire database:

> A good friend of mine and fellow board member is in the jewelry business. Jerry Menkin is very prominent in diamonds and high-end jewelry. Recently, Jerry started a campaign to support a charity that he has become actively involved in. He told me that he would provide the following services: appraisals, estate assessments, and minor repairs.
>
> He just asks that whatever he would charge for the service that the recipient of the service write a check directly to the charity.
>
> I had a diamond chip replaced in my wife's bracelet and was glad to make a donation.
>
> I thought you might have an interest in learning about this nice gesture; and if you have a need for any of these services, this is an opportunity to fulfill a need and do something good at the same time.
>
> If you are interested, please call Jerry directly.

The reason to do this is that Jerry is part of my team. He is as mindful of my needs as I am of his. By going a little out of the way for him I am helping one of my team players. I exposed Jerry to my database, thinking that there are always people who want these services. The difference is that they might feel a greater good knowing that they are helping a charity (which is also tax deductible) and doing something they had to get done anyway. Jerry feels good because he's aiding a pet cause; his clients feel good because they're helping a charity—and getting a service. I feel terrific because I helped form new relationships. Everyone wins, everyone is networking.

Jerry Menkin isn't earning any revenues on these services, but his upside is that he is creating new prospects. He has to think in terms of delayed gratification. His sales may not increase in the next few months, or even in the next year or two. These introductions may one day pay off, but he is smart enough to understand he has to be patient before hordes of new customers order new watches or diamond rings.

How does this help me? First, Jerry is appreciative because I've become an unusual type of fundraiser for his cause. Second, I am once again in front of my database with an idea that is completely unrelated to my business. This creates a positive impression, which could generate new business opportunities. The less it *looks* like you're trolling for new business, the better it is.

I also used this same technique to generate a charity event benefiting the American Diabetes Association. The sponsors were the New York Yankees and Sterling National Bank. (I'm on the board of the bank.) I sent out an e-mail to my entire database, asking interested recipients to contact the bank directly. Even though I directed the responses to the bank, I still received calls. Some contacts just wanted to thank me. Others reminded me that we haven't spoken for a while; a few wanted to get together to discuss a deal.

Here's another example: My friend has a restaurant that's doing all right, but he'd like to increase his business. He asked me, "How can we apply the power of your network to help me?" I immediately thought of a charitable tie-in, and told him that I knew someone who lost a young daughter to cancer. This girl was a real fighter, and I had empathy for her, so I approached her father and said, "I'd like to do something special. Why don't we do a wine-tasting at my friend's restaurant, charge $100 a head, and donate the proceeds to this foundation in her name." We're going to call it "A Wine Tasting That Makes a Difference." When I send out an e-mail with that heading along with a story about this young lady, I expect to get an enthusiastic response. I know I'll have hundreds of people who will be interested in this.

DATABASE AND NETWORKING TIP SHEET

➤ Always have your business cards with you. Simple enough, but I'm constantly surprised at how many people can't find theirs when they need them. Put them in an easily accessible pocket, so you don't have to fish through your wallet while you're talking to someone. This is always awkward and the sign of an inept networker. You don't have to present your card when you're introduced (as is the custom in Japan with "name" cards). But when someone asks, or you offer, it will always be at the ready, and you won't be fumbling for one.

➤ When you receive a business card, as soon as it's politely possible, make notes about the individual's business on the back of the card (and anything else that's pertinent from your conversation). Later, you should input that information into your database.

➤ If at all possible, send a follow-up e-mail saying what a pleasure it was to meet them. It should be short, perhaps mentioning a topic you connected on (so he or she will remember you), and suggest that you might get together at some future date.

➤ When you meet someone new, remember the person's name. Register that person in your mind. (I discussed the use of mnemonic devices in an earlier chapter. If you aren't good at this sort of thing—and many people are not—then I suggest you develop a method that works for you. Practice.) Embarrassing moments occur when you meet that person again, and have to introduce them to someone else and you don't remember his or her name. If this happens, you can casually say to your friend, "Tom, please introduce yourself." Usually, the person whose name you forgot will follow by introducing himself or herself. If that's not an option, I always favor direct honesty. "I'm terribly sorry, but I forgot your name." Try to avoid situations where you're constantly apologizing.

➤ Remembering birth dates is only appreciated when the person who remembers is a friend or there is some sort of a tangible relationship. Recording birthdays and sending cards to a mere acquaintance can be viewed as pretentious and insincere. Every year, I receive a birthday card from an insurance salesman who persisted in trying to sell me a policy. I have not spoken to him in five years. It's obvious that he sends cards to all prospects and this is his way of managing his database.

➤ Even with casual acquaintances, making a call or sending a card on a child's birth goes a long way. If you receive a birth announcement in the mail, send the appropriate gift.

➤ Send condolence cards, even to casual acquaintances. This type of gesture always goes a very long way. When I do it, I try to add a personal note if I knew the person at all. It's a thought from your heart, and it will make the aggrieved feel a little better.

Once you've established a reasonable command of your database, you can then begin to put your contacts to work.

Part Two

ADVANCED
NETWORKING

9

Use Networking to Create an Effective Network Group

Imagine that you are in a group of four businessmen who know each other really well and are employed in four totally different industries. Imagine that each of you is at the same level in your respective professions and that you are all very confident of each other's ability and integrity. In fact, each of you actively and routinely refers business and clients to one another. You know that sending business to each other will always be a win-win situation. The recipient of the introduction is always appreciative, and the referral is thankful to receive competent and first-class treatment. Imagine that the four of you conduct yourselves at the highest possible level of skill and integrity.

One day you collectively decide that since there is so much good business going on among the four of you that you should somehow leverage this nucleus into something larger. How do you accomplish this? Perhaps there should be some sort of formal meeting, even an organized meeting dedicated to increasing your networking web.

The four of you decide to meet once a month. The purpose of the meetings is to discuss new business opportunities, general business issues, and the economic climate, and to thank each other formally for business received.

Soon it becomes apparent that there is only so much business that can be derived from this foursome. The group is limited to its sphere of contacts due to its size.

A discussion ensues and you all decide that a fifth member is needed to increase business insights and breadth of contacts and to generate new opportunities. The new member, however, has to fit in. He has to be in a business that isn't a conflict with the existing members; and he has to demonstrate the same high level of integrity, enthusiasm, and unselfishness as the other members. This person has to have the right chemistry. Imagine there is a recruiting and acceptance process; and, in a short time, a fifth member is identified, interviewed, and asked to join your little group.

Congratulations. You and your friends have created a network group, and you are in the incipient stages of development.

Now imagine a year later that there are ten members, all of whom are in mutually exclusive businesses. Each member opens doors and creates business opportunities for the other members. Is this fantasy or reality? Unfortunately, the notion that each member is an expert in his or her field and that everybody refers business to each other is probably a bit unrealistic. Ideally, your networking group will grow and flourish. But if there are not enough nurturers, then the group itself could suffer. You must constantly evaluate each other's contributions.

Effective networking is a time-consuming endeavor and requires that the members understand that their payback may take quite a long time. Relationships are nurtured and introductions should not be made with a quid pro quo philosophy. It can be a relatively easy process, but it only works smoothly if you begin with the right core group and slowly and carefully add new people to the mix.

Each group member should strive to be the best individual networker he or she can be. I can't stress the importance of ensuring that each member of your group learns how to properly introduce people. Yes, it's basic, but it's also quantifiable in a way that will pay dividends.

Rule 19	"Frame" your contacts when introducing two people to each other.

Here's an example: When I was at a barbecue over the Fourth of July weekend, I noticed that two of my friends were there who didn't know each other. My friend Doug had owned Crunch, a New York City chain of gyms, and had sold it to Bally for many millions of dollars. The other friend, Mike, owns thirty Shop-Rite supermarkets in New Jersey. Both of them are accomplished, wealthy businessmen.

I decided to introduce them. "Doug, I want you to meet my friend Mike; Mike, I want you to meet Doug. You guys may find you have some things in common. Doug owned Crunch, the fitness chain. Mike owns several Shop-Rites in New Jersey." You might wonder, what do supermarkets and fitness gyms have in common? Nothing, perhaps, except the fact that these two men run businesses.

Doug and Mike talked for about an hour. Now, if I introduced them without mentioning their credentials, they might not have gotten into a deep conversation. I pushed the conversation along. I was selling each of them to each other. I frequently try to do this.

Why? Here are two smart, successful, interesting guys. First, I'm putting them together; that's what I do as a networker.

Second, I immediately announced their achievements. I just framed them both, and I put them in a position where there's instant respect for their business prowess. This is much more effective than introducing them without qualifiers. I just saved them fifteen or twenty minutes of dancing around with small talk until they wonder about the key question, "What do you do for a living?" Like it or not, our work defines us. And high-powered businesspeople are thinking about what they do all the time. Even at holiday barbecues.

Third, I was selling myself indirectly from far afield, because both are friends of mine, so both of them are thinking, "Jeff knows really interesting people, and he's putting all these successful people together." Later, they might introduce me to other accomplished people. So down the road, I'll meet people through them. So there are multiple agendas.

Fourth, and last, I *like* doing it. I sincerely like helping people. And it made me feel good that they sat there and spoke for an hour. I don't want—or expect—anything from them in return. The next day, Mike called me and said, "Do you have Doug's number, I want to give him a call." That call was the feel-good moment.

Most people will introduce someone and it just ends there. What I'm doing is facilitating the networking idea with something as simple as an introduction. The idea is not to wonder about where it will lead. That's a waste of networking energy.

For a networking group to be successful, you must get as many members as possible into the mind-set of making introductions, especially ones that may not seem logical at first. Sometimes a business contact can facilitate this by asking you for a favor. Whenever I'm talking with someone, I'm asking him or her all sorts of questions about what they do to connect them to the people that can help them with whatever their agendas are. I listen to whatever anyone says to me, and while I'm listening to him or her, I'm already thinking about whom to introduce them to.

I am not suggesting that everybody you meet is a potential networking candidate. You must be selective. Generally, your visceral sense is the best guide. There are very successful business people who are terrible networkers, and there are wonderful networkers who do not necessarily want to increase their business load. They're happy where they are. A good "group" networker has to want to ensure the group's success.

> **Rule 20**
>
> There is power in a team. Even the best networker can benefit from joining a networking group.

Successful networking groups start with a strong, committed membership. A robust membership develops when the group has a defined strategy, industry diversification, and a membership that consists of peer relationships. I want to caution you that it is essential that the membership be at a homogeneous level in the business hierarchy. For example, if you are a CEO of a company and you do business primarily with other CEOs, a group whose members are looking to meet human resource directors or facility managers would probably not be worthwhile.

The most important characteristic of a good networking group is trust among the membership. The hypothetical example in the beginning of this chapter is the goal. Respect, integrity, responsiveness, and high-level service are not hollow requirements. These are easily identifiable and often quantifiable traits. These characteristics should be the gold standard of the membership; when members fall short of the group's expectation, they should be asked to leave.

INEFFECTIVE GROUPS

If you are thinking of joining a group with a substantial history, you should be equally industrious about deciding whether a particular one meets your needs. There are many that are ineffective, and they exist in name only. Ineffective groups have members who do not have common interests; their meetings are sporadic and poorly planned; and they may be operated with conflicting agendas.

At one time I was a member of a networking group that was part of a consortium of ten other networking groups. The facilitator owned the networking organization and moderated all the various groups. Every week he had multiple meetings in multiple venues. He was so overwhelmed that the events became a worthless commodity. The meetings were simply not effective. The agendas were repetitive and not very stimulating. The members consisted of a few CEOs and mostly salesmen hungry for new leads.

Principally, the structure was flawed and diluted. The groups existed merely as a business, which is the worst reason to form a networking group. Why? There's an inherent conflict of interest. The facilitator wants to expand his business first and concern himself with networking synergy last. The business model required a new infusion of members at a steady rate, so quality control was nonexistent. The principal membership requirement was coming up with the $1,500 a year in dues, and naturally, the newly enlisted members compensated the facilitator. I attended meetings where some of the guests were so blatantly inappropriate that it became an embarrassment.

Rule 21   Only join not-for-profit network groups that are managed by the membership.

INCREASE YOUR BATTING AVERAGE

Baseball teams have coaches who help players perform better. A hitting coach concentrates on the fundamentals that will hopefully increase a batter's average or solve a hitch in his swing.

In networks, the members are a team and the facilitator or the leader of the group should assume the role of the coach.

Some members will be better at connecting people and bringing value than others will. The key questions are, "How do you get a member to improve his or her performance? How do you get this person to add to the inherent value in the process?"

Here is an example of how I was able to make a suggestion to a network group member who felt he was faltering. A friend of mine named Cliff, who brought me to the Metropolitan Business Network (a group that I'll go into more detail in the next chapter), was in something of a slump. He was complaining that he felt that he wasn't really getting any benefit by continuing as a member of the group and was considering resigning. I recognized this instantly as a good man in a temporary funk—not unlike a ballplayer who had a 2-for-30 week in the middle of August. It happens to all of us.

I called Cliff and suggested that we meet and discuss a plan of action. First, I suggested that he sift through his database and put together a list of ten people who are either owners of companies or highly regarded businesspeople and then forward the list to me. I told him that we will analyze each of these individuals, and I will recommend introducing them or perhaps inviting them to be a guest at the group's next meeting.

Several days later, when I received his list, at least eight of ten people were easily the types who could possibly become valuable members of the Metropolitan Business Network. Also, I introduced someone on his list to a contact of mine, and Cliff was already involved in it. Cliff followed my advice, and two of the people on the list actually became members.

Suddenly, his attitude changed. There were hugely helpful contacts in his database, and he was no longer desensitized to them. More business opportunities emerged, and Cliff became enthusiastic. It didn't take long for him to re-groove his swing.

Rule 22

"Pick up" valuable group members who experience temporary slumps. The group as a whole will benefit from his resurgence.

This exercise works well and is an effective way to stimulate someone who has temporary doubts about his networking ability. We all have active databases, and sometimes an objective third party can be very helpful in ascertaining the value of who we know. When operating a network group the facilitator or the strongest member should use this method for members who they feel are ineffective but can still contribute to the organization.

INDIRECT NETWORKING

In *Robert's Rules,* a book by Mark Roberts, the author describes a very effective way to build a database. Roberts's life is a bit more glamorous than most because he is one of the most well-known promoters of athletic and entertainment talent. He started his career representing young boxers. Early on, he realized that at every boxing match the people in the crowd were ardent fans of the sport. This realization did not take much intellectual capital on Roberts's part. But he was shrewd: He understood that in a single arena there were hundreds of people who lived and dreamed boxing. Roberts decided he wanted to know all of them.

If they were attending this fight, they likely would be interested in future events.

Cleverly, Mark hired attractive women to canvas the audience and hand out short questionnaires. He wanted to learn where people lived, what they did for a living, what kinds of shows they liked, and how often they went. To guarantee a good response he offered incentives to both the questionnaire-takers and the fans. The woman with the most completed surveys received a cash award. The fans who filled out the card would have a chance to win a great raffle.

Over the years his database grew to more than fifteen thousand names. He would send out mailings of his major events and faxes about his company to people who were later qualified as real enthusiasts. This method of indirect networking can be very effective. In Roberts's case he was able to get his customers excited and had no trouble selling tickets. Roberts's company eventually went public. In addition to becoming a good businessman, he became a great networker by executing a simple plan to build his audience.

DRILL-DOWN DAY

My networking group recently instituted a new, advanced exercise that has become quite valuable. Suggested by Howard Schwartz, a businessman who owned an institutional trading firm that he later sold to Instinet, this exercise has helped members become better acquainted, and has produced new levels of trust and commitment to the group. We eventually called Schwartz's idea Drill-down Day. It is certainly the kind of day that new groups could benefit from when they achieve a certain level of critical mass. It helped us all become more enthusiastic and embrace the power of what we're trying to create with this platform.

On Drill-down Day, the members spend a full day all but locked in a conference room together. We're all expected to be there the whole day, and there are no distractions. Absolutely no cell phones, which should say something about its serious nature. We all have to make the commitment of total concentration. Basically, every member has to make a presentation. It can be about anything, but it usually centers on the person's life, accomplishments, dreams, and aspirations. People come with PowerPoint presentations with slides of their childhood. The types of stories they told about how they feel about themselves are quite revealing. Several members actually spend a lot of time preparing their presentations. Occasionally, members give speeches that border on confessionals. I suppose mine was like that.

When it was my turn to take the podium, I shared with the room a short summary of where I came from, how I spent my youth, my early struggles, jobs where I learned more than I earned, and so on. I think my underprivileged background particularly touched the audience. By this, I mean emotionally and psychologically, not so much financially.

My parents were divorced when I was five, they remarried each other when I was fifteen, then they divorced again ten years later. My mother was a problem drinker, and her family lost all their money. When I was a child, she threatened to kill herself. I saw things that I clearly should not have seen as a boy. My mother was a very attractive woman, so she was a revolving door in terms of men coming in and out of our apartment. As I mentioned earlier in the book, my father owned gas stations, but he eventually lost all his money, too. I took care of my mother, and then I had to take care of my father as he got older.

I remember watching TV shows like *Leave It to Beaver,* and *The Donna Reed Show,* and thinking, "Why can't my life be like that? Why can't I have a family life that's wholesome and loving and normal?" I was reveling in these shows, thinking how nice for my life to be like the Cleavers'. To some extent, my emotionally difficult household steered me in the right direction; and it toughened me and made me strong.

My background was hardly unique, but it was certainly atypical as far as our group was concerned. I either could have crumbled and gone down a bad path (certainly it would have been understandable); but instead, I resolved not to end up like either of my parents. My childhood was so devoid of the normal kind of love and affection that it inspired me to become more resilient, hardworking, and eventually successful. I used my story as an inspirational tool.

It's important to remember that Drill-down Day does not produce immediate rewards for group members. It is not meant to be a business meeting of any kind. What it does is bring individual members closer together, and it develops a level of trust and friendship that later helps us in our business lives. It is a way to open yourself up, to get people to understand who you are and where you come from. Drill-down Day helps us uncover ourselves, builds our characters, and enhances our social beings. All this, we believe, leads to becoming a better-connected businessman. This trust-building exercise is second to none.

10

The Dynamics of Running a Network

I truly believe there is a science—however inexact—of keeping a successful networking group powerful. It's something that requires a lot of thought from its members and a steady and creative input of energy and new ideas. Ideally, the members have to feel a devout passion for the platform. The meetings have to be fresh, moving, insightful, and attended by guests who can bring value. A networking group is organic, and it is constantly evolving. How it evolves has to do with the intellectual capital and effort of its lifeblood—the members themselves.

Many small business groups don't understand what it takes to form a team that networks its members. Their meetings are loose, disjointed, and unfocused, and, in many cases, attended by individuals whose orientation is geared principally toward aggressive solicitation. It's essential to fully understand what works and what doesn't.

GET RIGHT TO THE POINT—BREVITY RULES THE WORLD OF CONTACTS

There is a group called the International Executive Resource Group, or IERG. It has a membership of more than three hundred individuals, all of whom held senior positions at internationally based companies, mostly Fortune 100 firms. Many members served in venues such as India or China or Britain, all over the world. I was asked to speak to the group, and the day I appeared, there were about sixty people in the room. One was formerly the CEO of Eastman Kodak's metal division in Great Britain. Another was head of sales for IBM's laptop division in China. And so on. These men and women all were experienced businesspeople, but they were now all looking for jobs.

But at the meeting, I realized that while all these people came from a sophisticated corporate environment, they had an extremely narrow view of the networking world. Mostly, they had lived in a world of corporate executives, replete with the commensurate business perks. Few had been out on their own, functioning as entrepreneurs, meeting a payroll, lying awake at night, worrying about where their business was going. Perhaps they had a list of contacts, but it was narrow casted, skewed toward their specialty. Few had ever had the need to become real rainmakers, real networkers. Their mentality was that they were the hubs of the wheel, and people looking for business always solicited them—not the other way around. They had probably burned bridges in the past, and now that they were in transition— or more bluntly, out of work—they were no longer the hubs. Just shaky spokes in the wheel. Now they were the ones hoping someone in power would take their phone calls.

Before I even addressed the group, I discovered a sense of desperation in the room. The attendees were so hungry to find jobs that they did not have a good sense of how they were selling themselves. I knew they hadn't organized or updated their databases; indeed, if they even had them at all. I knew they had no sense of collecting business cards and putting them to use by carefully organizing and amending them.

At the end of my speech, I mentioned that anyone could chat with me, and I'd be glad to listen to what they do and to help open up some doors. The following day, I received about seventy résumés via e-mail. Well, I wasn't going to read everyone's curriculum vitae. I didn't have the bandwidth to do it, nor the interest. So I began thinking, "These executives really don't have any idea how to organize themselves. They barrage people with their résumés, and people just don't read résumés."

So the next day, I called up the fellow who ran the organization, and I said, with my usual directness, "I hope you aren't offended by my being so forward, but I don't think your group is anywhere near as effective as it should be. I came up with an idea for your group. For what I believe will be a very effective marketing tool. If you agree, and you do what I suggest, I will take that tool, and I will send it out to my database."

He was still listening. I asked him to put together two pieces of paper for me. And on the two pieces of paper, I wanted the following headings: CEO, CIO, COO, CFO, CTO, Head of Sales, Senior VP, and so on. I was careful to warn him that under those headings, I didn't want names, addresses, e-mail addresses. I didn't want to know how many dogs these people had, or where they lived, or how many kids they had, or their weekend hobbies. All I wanted to know was, for example, if under CEO, you had that gentleman from Eastman Kodak. Then you would put him under CEO: The listing would read, "Eastman Kodak, Metal Division, Great Britain." And then you had the guy who was head of sales for IBM. He'd be listed under the Head of Sales category, "IBM, Laptop Division, China."

When he was finished, I was going to have a list of fifty former CEOs, forty-nine former CFOs, forty-nine former Head of Sales—a very succinct list, based on their affiliation. I then sent out that list to my database with the following note:

"I recently had the pleasure to speak in front of a very engaging, very accomplished group of business professionals that were associated with Fortune 100 companies at the most senior of levels. All these individuals are currently looking to buy a company, reside on a board, and/or get back into the game. I thought I'd share this list with everyone in my database, and if there's anyone who would like to meet any of these individuals, I'd be glad to facilitate an introduction."

I received 250 responses. Two people were hired as CEOs from it. Some people wound up on boards. And then I got calls from people, like a lawyer in Florida, who said to me, "Jeff, this is such a great idea; this is amazing. Do you mind if I send it out to my database?" I said, "Mind? Of course not. It makes you look good—you're going out of your way, you're trying to connect people." He did it. He got an excellent rate of response.

I have been asked, "Why do you do these things? Why do you go out of your way?" My answer is, "Think about it for a second. First of all, the effort was nominal. The others did all the work. All I did was write a little paragraph, I pushed the send button on my computer, and it went out to all these people. Also, the fact that all this good stuff happened means that all these accomplished people that had great affiliations probably think well of me. In the future, when I send them something via e-mail, they're going to read it. And perhaps if they hear of a financing deal, or a financial transaction, they will give me a call. I've created opportunity, and if nothing comes my way, I enjoyed doing it anyway. I did the right thing. And, in the end, I created a positive perception of myself."

VETTING THE MEMBERSHIP—AND HELPING MEMBERS STAY MOTIVATED

It would seem glaringly obvious that to be part of a good network you need good members. What is expected from someone to be a good member? It is sometimes very difficult to predict whether a member will be effective and will contribute. The board and the existing members try to ascertain commitment by asking some perfunctory questions during the admissions process. The three basic questions commonly asked are:

- ➤ Will you attend meetings?
- ➤ Will you introduce other members to your business contacts?
- ➤ Will you bring qualified guests?

Of course, prospective members always say yes; however, many don't deliver. I often reflect on why some individuals perform worse than others do and have concluded that reasons range from selfishness to simply not understanding the power of the team. Me-oriented thinkers are usually suspect when it comes to networking skills, and in many cases, are too selfish to be taught. Whereas, the better performer is sensitive to others' needs, is a long-term thinker, and will always consider the possibilities.

Rule 23   Engage in we-thinking and not me-thinking.

The basic questions for a potential network member are better framed in this manner:

- ➤ How serious are you about making a commitment—in both time and energy—to this group?
- ➤ Will you be generous in making introductions between the group and your business associates?
- ➤ Do you have enough contacts in your business circle to

bring guests who may have a significant impact on our group, and possibly even join at some point?

Some of the answers to these questions might be self-evident by the individual's degree of success. What isn't obvious, however, is the willingness to share.

Some of my fellow board members emphasize the company over the individual. Their theory is that big-name companies automatically produce great members. This is a dangerous assumption when it comes to building a networking group. In practice, the size of the company does not matter; it is always the individual who participates at the meetings who distinguishes a good member from a bad member. I've seen terrific people from small firms and terrible ones from large firms. There seems to be no particular pattern.

At one time Turner Construction was a member of the Metropolitan Business Network and one of their senior executives was the participant in the group. Turner is a highly regarded construction management firm with substantial building projects all over the country. One would think that it would be a real advantage to have a company like this one represented in your group. It's the equivalent to landing a Wal-Mart as an anchor tenant in a shopping center. But the reality was that the firm was a significant underperformer. The senior executive representing Turner rarely attended meetings. He was remiss in returning phone calls and wasn't great in making introductions. Perhaps a different senior executive from Turner would have been a better choice.

After many years of being on the board of a networking group, I have learned many of the key principles of evaluating a potential member.

If you already are a part of a group or you're considering starting one, you should consider the following points when evaluating new applicants:

> Did the person go out on his or her own to meet with the membership? If you have to prod the individual, then he really isn't interested enough.

> After the applicant met with members, did he make any introductions? It may seem presumptuous to assume that after a single meeting the individual will begin to make introductions. However, if they do, it's already a positive sign. I often make introductions after I meet somebody for the first time. Some people believe that you take a big risk by introducing someone you don't know. The fear is understandable because the person is thinking, *"What happens if it doesn't work out? They will blame me. It probably isn't worth it."* Many times I have had advisers tell me that making introductions is a no-win situation. If something good comes from it, the client won't appreciate it; and if something goes wrong, they will take the blame. This type of thinking is just wrong, narrow-minded, and completely contrary to the basic precepts of networking.

When I introduce someone I only know casually, but have a positive gut sense of his personality, I generally qualify the introduction by saying that I *believe* there is the possibility for synergy between the two of you.

Rule 24

Don't be hesitant to introduce two people who appear to have synergy. If your gut feeling is positive, go with it. Savvy businessmen will vet each other's credentials on their own.

Essentially, I make the introduction with disclaimers and mitigate the risk to me if it doesn't work out. If you're candid when you introduce people, then both parties will remember it.

➤ Does the prospective member have a credible background? Is he well regarded in the business world? (Finding out what boards and charities the person serves on is usually a good indicator of how much outside energy and time the applicant will have for your group. The very best performers have an insatiable appetite for this kind of work, and the "busiest" people often are able to make time for additional causes without complaining.)

➤ Does he or she have a reputation for delivering quality service?

➤ Is the applicant in a position to make valuable referrals to other group members?

➤ Does the applicant voice his or her opinions? Will he make suggestions to improve the group or help it run more smoothly and efficiently?

MONITORING THE MEMBERSHIP ON A CONTINUING BASIS

Being a member of a networking group is like being a member of a team. In baseball, the individual's batting average, RBIs, on-base percentage, and how well he fields his position are the criteria that distinguish a great player from a mediocre one.

In networking groups, the evaluation starts with attendance at the meetings, contribution by bringing valuable guests, business contacts introduced, and business conduct.

On a baseball team, there are the heavy hitters (the top of the order and cleanup), and then there are the average and light hitters that bat eighth or ninth. In networking groups, there are a few cleanup hitters and many average batters. The group's effectiveness is predicated upon making trades or not renewing members that don't contribute. The board must formulate definitive rules and membership criteria.

The process of not renewing a member can be difficult and at times awkward. It is essential that the members understand the expectations and obligations of the group. If they are not performing to the mandated standards, there should be a methodology in place whereby they are met with and advised of their subpar performance. If they do not raise the level of their contribution within an agreed amount of time, then they should not be renewed. Interestingly enough, the very person who has not attended meetings and has shown an overall lack of interest may be extremely disappointed when asked to leave the group. Hopefully, the warning meeting will mitigate hard feelings.

BOARD MEETINGS

If a member accepts a board position, he or she has to be a cleanup hitter. It is a much greater commitment, and the individual has to really understand the dynamics of networking. Prior to every meeting, we conduct a board meeting. We plan the agenda, evaluate the membership, and are constantly trying to think of ways to improve our overall performance.

The board carefully monitors the members' performance. If a member misses multiple meetings and isn't contributing, the member is asked to come to a future board meeting to discuss their performance.

I am proud to say that my networking group—the Strategic Forum—has become a paradigm of a flourishing, well-managed organization.

THE STRATEGIC FORUM (SOUTH FLORIDA CHAPTER)

It's very funny how things sometimes develop in life. I move to Florida and start commuting back and forth. When I'm there, I spend my time running around meeting people, shaking hands, and developing relationships.

I started collecting some great talent. Florida is full of entrepreneurs who sold their companies and now are looking for a lifestyle that's better. I decided to throw a dinner forum and sort of created a similar venue as the Strategic Forum in New York. Morton's had a great private room and on three separate occasions I organized this event. One of the guests introduced me to his brother, Seth Werner.

About a year and a half ago, Seth Werner came to New York and attended one of our meetings. Seth was formerly CEO and founder of Mortgate.com and is currently the CEO of Cypress Creek Capital, a company affiliated with Bank Atlantic in South Florida.

Seth, a former "YPO-er" (Young Republican Organization), was really taken by the dynamics of our meeting. In fact, he coined the phrase "the Strategic Forum is YPO on steroids." Seth suggested to me that we have to start a chapter in South Florida and that he would like to be a founder with me. I was considering a Florida branch, but I definitely needed help to make it happen. Shortly thereafter Seth called me. He took it on his own to contact Dr. Randy Pohlman, the dean of the Nova Business School. Seth was able to convince Randy to have the school donate its brand-new conference room for our meetings. The give-back to the school would be that once we had a significant membership, students would be able to audit our meetings and learn about networking as a curriculum add-on for the first time in a collegiate setting. I said to myself, *Wow!*

Seth created a nucleus around five individuals, including myself, to be on the board and turned this idea into a reality. One year later, we have twenty-five members. Their résumés are truly impressive—i.e., former president of Continental Airlines, former CEO of Office Depot, former CEO of GNC, publisher of *The Miami Herald,* and two prominent authors to name a few. The business transactions that had been introduced have been substantive.

One example that resonates with me involves an introduction that I created. I was introduced by one of our members to a gentleman named Bob Diener. Interestingly, Bob and his partner started a small travel company with $1,200 and, ultimately, sold it. You may be familiar with it: Hotels.com. Anyway, coincidence would have it that Michael Rapp, the chairman of Broadband (a New York Strategic Forum member), was retained by a company in China (Elong) that happens to be in the same space as Hotels.com, and Michael was engaged to raise $15 million to fund growth.

During my meeting, I mentioned Elong to Bob, thinking there may be a synergy. I created the introduction. E-mails ensued, and a year and a half later Barry Diller's company, which acquired Hotels.com, bought Elong, which ultimately turned a $100-million-plus transaction.

Twenty students filled out applications for the South Florida chapter and wrote an essay to participate. Fifteen were picked. The meetings were lively, and students learned some things they were not taught before.

The alliance with Nova University has been so successful that we currently are talking to some New York universities to create a similar dynamic. Recently, a good friend of mine was so impressed by our group dynamics that we are planning to start a chapter in Philadelphia.

The group is now accomplished enough that a new member begins with a "provisional" membership, which typically lasts a year. This is not our arrogance showing; it's merely a way to send a message that you're expected to be an active contributor. If you're not, you're not helping yourself or anyone else, and you'll be asked to leave.

THE FACILITATOR AND THE ADMINISTRATOR— TWO KEYS TO AN EFFECTIVE NETWORKING GROUP

One of the more difficult tasks is to find an individual who can both run the meeting well and nurture the membership. Since the members all have their own businesses, it is ideal if there is a paid facilitator. The facilitator's skill set should include having an outgoing personality, being well organized, and being sensitive to monitoring the members' performance. The facilitator should periodically meet with each member and gather his or her opinions and issues about the group's performance. The administrator performs the housekeeping chores (e-mails, scheduling, news, and so on), and the board delegates to the administrator all the day-to-day operations of the group.

An effective facilitator would know how to prepare and lead guest presentations as well as to cut them off when the guest is speaking too long or is not on point or stimulating. If a member is ineffective or isn't meeting the expectations of the group, the facilitator should be dispatched to motivate the member. However, in most cases an unmotivated member generally doesn't get better. Remember that the facilitator is paid by the group and should be directed by the board. A facilitator who insists on doing things his own way is not serving the board or the members and should be replaced.

MINIMEETINGS HELP MEMBERS STAY CURRENT

At the Metropolitan Business Network, we frequently break the group into minimeetings. These meetings are in addition to the regular meetings. Usually a minimeeting will involve six to eight members, but it can be as few as three or four. (The number of participants doesn't matter, *if* the meetings are run properly, if there's a facilitator that makes sure that you're pulling people out, that you're getting them to speak, and that you're engaging people so that nobody is left out. That's why a facilitator is beyond essential to make a group work.) These smaller groups facilitate an open and more intimate give-and-take between the members. Individual members can articulate what they are getting from the group. It can also be a forum to critique how the network is generally working. Whoever is running the minimeeting (generally a board member) records all the observations and reports this information at the next board meeting. Minimeetings are a great way for a member to air grievances and to suggest improvements. The dynamics and interaction in a smaller group are more intimate and provide an opportunity for individual members to get to know each other better. Generally it is a good idea to select the attendees of the minimeetings from dissimilar business categories. Network groups have a tendency to break up in cliques where business synergies exist. The minimeetings are an opportunity to cross-pollinate among members who usually don't interact.

PREPARING GUEST SPEAKERS

One of the best ways to keep your membership engaged and motivated is to schedule luncheon or meeting speakers who are dynamic at the podium. It's important to opt for candidates who are good presenters, rather than to simply invite name speakers who may not be motivated to prepare crisp, clear, well-organized presentations.

There is a reason the heads of major corporations have speechwriters. There is a reason that CEOs—and other senior managers—of public companies hire expensive training consultants to teach them the rudiments of presentation and speaking skills. Surprisingly, many successful people present poorly. One reason is that they've never taken the time to learn how to reach hundreds, or even thousands, in a single audience. Why? It's not on the list of executive skill sets, and it's probably not a priority at Wharton or Harvard Business School. (In fact, I know of only one course in speechwriting, which is taught at the graduate level at Columbia.) These people are so busy climbing the corporate ladder that they never wonder whether they can speak effectively in front of a large group. It's just not a requirement of a high-level job description, though after watching dozens of terrible speakers drone on for hours, I think it should be.

At one of my network group's meetings, all our guests are briefed in advance by their host. We want to be sure he or she knows what our audience is interested in and that they should stay on message. Despite hearing this sermon, when the curtain goes up some guests still speak ineffectively. A group must have somebody that leads the guest during their presentation and frames or steers them to maximize their effect on the room.

Recently, I invited a guest who was a pioneer in the cell phone industry and is currently a venture capitalist. I told him that when he presented he should tell the story of the genesis of the cell phone and then elaborate on what he is looking for now. I told him to be prepared to answer tough, probing questions.

Instead, he gave his audience an itemized list of all his investments over the years. There was no story line, and the atmosphere in the room was deflating. I immediately jumped in and said, "Irv, excuse me. I have had the pleasure of knowing you for quite a while. I am amazed at your foresight and know in detail some of your successful experiences. Isn't it true that you were one of the first guys who attempted to commercialize cellular phone technology?"

He said yes and began telling the story about how cell phones became a product. The energy in the room instantly materialized, and everybody was fixated on the presentation. As he was wrapping up, I turned to Sam Klein and said, "Sam, you sold your company to Nextel. Did you have a similar experience?"

An open conversation ensued among several of the participants who were telecom entrepreneurs. All the other members listened intently. The insights were fascinating. Keeping the room moving is essential, especially when you have a speaker who isn't up to the task. One of the board members needs to take the lead in this role.

SPOTLIGHT PRESENTATIONS

There are two types of spotlight presentations. Periodically, we will invite an outside speaker who is prominent in business or politics to give a broad, personal view on a timely topic. The other kind of spotlight presentation typically features an existing member who takes to the podium. This is an opportunity for the member to highlight his business graphically for the entire membership. When there are thirty members, it can be very difficult for each member to understand the other twenty-nine members' businesses. The spotlight updates all the members about changes in the presenter's business. It also highlights how business finds its way into the presenter's company. It is an excellent way to help the group understand how they can be of value to the spotlight member's business. Lastly, each member at the podium often gives a surprisingly accurate picture of the larger economy's ebbs and flows. Often, these snapshots are better indicators of what's to come than the many pundits who are quoted in the nation's business media.

THE ANNUAL CHRISTMAS EVENT

It is important to put some fun in your work, especially your networking work. Every year our networking group has a holiday party, and it is one that makes a difference. In addition to being a relaxing and happy affair, it is also very productive. The board picks a member who has been an outstanding contributor to the group during the year and asks him to choose a New York–based charity he has a particular affection for. Essentially, a productive member is being rewarded for all of his or her efforts.

The board asks the entire membership to reach out to their contacts to solicit donations for prizes to be auctioned off. The items have ranged from airline tickets to free dinners at prominent restaurants. One year, I came up with an offbeat raffle idea: The members would submit a picture of themselves as a child. The pictures were numbered and placed on a large easel. Members filled out a ballot, guessing which picture aligned with each member. The one who had the most correct guesses won a pair of airline tickets. The Christmas event is a nice way to end a productive year.

THE YEAR-END REVIEW AND TALLY

During the last regular meeting of the year of the Metropolitan Business Network, all of the members are asked to recall business created through introductions from the group. They are also asked to specifically acknowledge the individual who introduced that business to them and the total revenues received for the year. Every year since I have been a member the amount has increased. Last year, the total reported was $20 million. Formal networking really works.

11

Networking Groups in Action

Despite a lingering skepticism, I joined my first formal networking group, the Metropolitan Business Network (MBN), in the early 1990s. I was wary about joining a networking group, because I had dabbled with others in the past and they were disappointing. They were loosely organized, and most of the members were middle managers and salespeople looking to sell. The energy necessary to propagate contacts just wasn't there. The prevailing attitude was simply: Here is my business card, what can you do for me?

So when I was invited to an MBN meeting, I thought I'd give it one more try. Perhaps this one was different. I was asked to make a presentation about my company. After I had finished explaining the details of my business, I had to be prepared to answer questions.

Meetings were held at 8:00 A.M. every other Thursday. Thirty-plus people, all of whom represented different companies and industries, were usually present. The first half hour was an informal chat session, where members gradually filled the room. Here, guests were typically walked around the room and introduced. The first member I met was David Gensler, the president of Madison Pension. A decade later, we are close friends and often involved in business deals together. Members and guests often exchanged business cards before the meeting started.

The president usually began by discussing some relevant network items and then asked the membership to introduce themselves. Each member took a minute or less to greet the group. Cliff Broder, my banker and sponsor at my first meeting, said, "I am Cliff Broder, senior vice president of Republic National Bank. Republic is a full service commercial bank whose main focus is the business needs of midmarket companies." At that first meeting, the introductions took about ten to fifteen minutes. I began jotting down the names of the people I wanted to meet.

ACKNOWLEDGING THE REFERRALS FROM WITHIN THE GROUP

After the introductions were finished, one of the board members stood up and explained the next part of the meeting called Thank-yous. He emphasized there is no monetary compensation paid among the members for business referrals or contacts. The only currency is recognition by way of a thank-you in front of the group. Thank-yous are given for business that happened or introductions to potential opportunities and not for house calls or personal favors. I remember wondering to myself what were these things called house calls.

The president announced, "Okay, let's get started."

Promptly, at least ten members raised their hands. Each member had another member to thank and, in some cases, a member had six or seven thank-yous. Some of the thank-yous were clearly for some really meaningful business opportunities and consummated transactions. This session lasted for about fifteen minutes. I was amazed at how much business was being initiated by the members for each other. What was even more astonishing was the number of the thank-yous announced because only two weeks had elapsed since their last meeting.

GUEST INTRODUCTIONS

After the thank-yous were finished, the next phase of the agenda was the guest presentations. I was the first speaker called.

"Good morning, my name is Jeffrey Meshel," I began. "I am the president of Mercury Capital. Mercury Capital is a fully integrated mortgage and real estate investment company. On the lending side, we are a resource to real estate owners that need funding quickly. Mercury can close a transaction in one week. Speed is our service; we are bridge lenders, which means that we lend short term (usually one year) and charge higher than conventional rates.

"You might ask yourself why would a transaction have to close so quickly. Most of the deals we close are either solving a problem or facilitating an opportunity. Sometimes a conventional lender backs out at the last minute. Rather than lose the deal and possibly an expensive contract deposit the borrower comes to us.

"We also are real estate investors. Mercury actively buys property, and we manage our own portfolio."

The questions began. "Your business sounds very interesting. Who are your clients?"

"I interact mostly with company owners and CEOs. Due to the nature of the business I have relationships with executives in virtually every industry."

Another hand immediately went up. "How do you think you could be helpful to the room? Would you make introductions?"

I thought for a moment before I answered, and I realized that I always introduced people that I felt comfortable with.

"The breadth of my clientele is vast. I am sure that I could contribute to the meetings by bringing interesting guests. In time, as I become knowledgeable about each member's business, I would be glad to make introductions."

The president stood up and called for one last question. "If you become a member, would you be the attending member from your company?" (The MBN's membership policy allows for a primary member and an associate member from each company. In many cases, the primary member did not often attend, but I did not know that then.) I answered affirmatively, and perhaps sensing my enthusiasm, I was immediately invited to join the group.

It was clear that the network could become an unpaid sales force. Consider the group's structure for a moment: You have members who are in a variety of services and product businesses, none of which are competing with each other. For example, we have a member who is from a company in the copier distribution business, and another is in the office supply business. By their very nature, they have opportunities on a daily basis to sell to the same clients. They can exchange lists of contacts and leads; there's a natural symbiosis.

BUSINESS IN PROGRESS

Once again, a board member stood up and explained the agenda. "This part of the meeting is an opportunity for anyone who is working on a particular piece of business to reach out to the membership and to ask for assistance or an introduction.

"You will notice on your table that there are lists of companies submitted by members of Allied Office Products and Leslie Digital. If you need help, please give a list prior to the meeting to Patty (the facilitator) who will make copies and will circulate the list for the meeting. Allied and Leslie have their lists on the table, so let's start with them."

Both Allied and Leslie were very prolific in presenting a list. Allied sold office products and Leslie Digital sold copiers. Virtually any company could be their customer.

A moment went by while the membership read over the lists and then hands shot up.

"Avery [Leslie Digital representative], who are you dealing with at Seagram?"

"We have a proposal in front of Bill Daly, a senior vice president. There are two other companies vying for the business," he said.

"I know the CEO. Call me later. I will see what I can do."

Another response came quickly. "Kaye, Scholer [a large New York city law firm] is one of my clients. Who are you dealing with there?"

If each list had ten companies on it, the membership knew or had a contact with half of them. This was truly an amazing percentage.

After Leslie Digital and Allied Office Products lists were finished, other members raised their hands seeking a wide range of assistance.

I raised my hand. "One of my areas of interest is to be introduced to banks or financial institutions that may have defaulted mortgages," I said. "There are times that they prefer to sell bad paper rather than go through the entire foreclosure process. If anybody knows a senior person in such an institution I would appreciate an introduction." Two hands went up. I jotted down the names of the members who had offered to help.

After the meeting, Cliff explained to me the procedure of becoming a member. First, I needed to do a series of these mysterious things called house calls. House calls are one-to-one meetings with members. The purpose is to get to know one another and to learn more about each other's business. These one-to-ones are a key ingredient to creating relationships and making a network group effective.

I considered whether I wanted to devote the time to being part of this group. I concluded that if the proper time was devoted to it, working these new relationships certainly would produce new business opportunities.

The first house call I had was with one of the founding members. Gene Fink was president of Winfield Security, a security guard and investigation firm. Gene was very friendly and responsive when I called, and he invited me to his office the following day. The conversation went something like this.

"Gene, you've been involved in this group since its inception," I said. "Has it been a beneficial experience?"

"I would honestly tell you that a large percentage of our business has come from referrals received from the members of the group. In fact, our biggest client, Fleet Bank, was an introduction from Goldstein Golub Kessler, our member in the accounting slot. I'm very committed to the group. It does require time, but like anything else in life, you get out what you put into it."

"I was very impressed by the thank-you session of the meeting. It seemed like a lot of business was being conducted through membership introductions. I'm assuming some companies fare better than others?" I asked.

"I am sure that's true," he said. "But the more involved members probably receive more. As an example, I've always directed a lot of referrals to Goldstein Golub Kessler. As a result, they became sensitive to what I do. One day Fleet, a client of theirs, called them and asked if they had a good resource for security guards."

"Sounds like a quid quo pro," I said.

"Not really. I've received referrals from other members and have given business to other members without it going both ways."

Over the next half hour we discussed our businesses and what we were looking for. I left the meeting thinking that Gene was a team player and that I would be well off joining his team.

I had four or five house calls, and each member was different. All of them espoused the merits of the group and the benefits they received. I was convinced I wanted to join. At the time, protocol required that I would be invited back to present once again. In the two-week gap between meetings, I went out of my way to introduce members I met to people I thought were synergistic to their business. During thank-yous, several members formally thanked me and one actually closed a deal. The board would confer on my nomination at the next meeting, and after polling some of the members I found that they would vote on my admission into the group.

I was a maniacal networker and advocate of the group's generosity in introductions. Six months later, I was asked to join the board of directors and ever since have helped in steering the direction of the group. The Metropolitan Business Network actually morphed into becoming part of my business. I thought about it, worked hard, and made an effort to improve it every day. The platform became a valuable component of my business and leveraged my skill sets.

There is an art in running an effective group. Thirty members with different desires, opinions, and abilities require a lot of attention. Somehow networking became second nature to me, and I found myself constantly thinking of ways to make the group stronger.

I was a member of the MBN for ten years before I started The Strategic Forum. I can unequivocally say that being part of this group has created a multitude of business opportunities for me. There was an additional benefit; it made me a better businessman.

THE STRATEGIC FORUM

It wasn't long before I became anointed as a competent networker. But as I saw how formal groups added value to the business proposition of all kinds of companies, I also saw a need to expand my contact list even more. I decided to begin my own networking group, The Strategic Forum.

The mission of The Strategic Forum is to provide a venue where productive and powerful business leaders from a broad range of industries meet to exchange ideas and introduce relationships that create opportunities. Members are expected to bring value to the forum, and they feel privileged to be included. Presentations by interesting and knowledgeable guests with a similar orientation provide fresh insight and generate new opportunities. The Forum is particularly rewarding because its shared intellectual capital combined with the business and personal relationships foster a very powerful bond.

Kary Presten, my cofounder, had an idea. Long Island City, which is contiguous to New York City, has hundreds of large companies that are members of an organization called the Long Island City Business Development Corporation. The LICBDC is a local organization that represents business interests in the community. If your garbage isn't being picked up or you are unhappy with a broken traffic light, you can call the LICBDC. Occasionally, the organization has events where local politicians discuss regional issues.

Membership benefits included a newsletter, periodic breakfast seminars, and a database of virtually every business and its owner in the surrounding area. The membership list is very impressive. However, the organization did not have a platform that promoted business or interaction among its members.

Kary suggested that we join LICBDC and attempt to start a network group. The association had no problem with us approaching its membership to form our own group, separate and apart from the LICBDC. (Initially we called ourselves The Five Business Borough Network, in retrospect, a truly awful name. Luckily, the name didn't last but the group endured.) Our plan was to attract a diverse group of business owners situated throughout the city's boroughs. It took almost three years to put the key players in place.

Currently, The Strategic Forum has twenty-five members. All are owners of companies, CEOs, or entrepreneurs in transition. Monthly meetings are held in U.S. Trust's boardroom. The membership always invites six to eight guests. There is a waiting list. All the guests are accomplished business executives or entrepreneurs with similar disciplines to those of the membership, but are not conflicting. Generally, there is a spotlight speaker, echoing the format of the Metropolitan Business Network. Usually, this speaker is a noted authority in some business or political position.

Twice a year we have a cocktail party at a tony venue instead of a regular meeting. The membership is obligated to invite high-caliber guests. This event allows everyone to mingle informally and hopefully meet someone who will be a source of new business.

Where our methodology differs from the other networking groups is in our extensive preparation. All the guests are required to submit a short business biography. This information, which includes the referring member, is collated. When the final guest list is assembled it is e-mailed to all the guests and members prior to the meeting. The purpose is to inform the guests of who is coming so they can identify people they want to meet. Many guests work the room with the list in hand. And because everyone has seen it before the party, the electricity and level of connection is outstanding.

At regular meetings, we break into an open discussion about the economy. Since we are in what many CEOs call challenging times, the shared insights are invaluable.

Once, a suburban real estate developer was making a presentation. This man owned several shopping centers and was discussing the dynamics of the retail market in upstate New York.

He mentioned that the following day he would be signing a contract on a parcel in Westchester across the street from a major shopping center with a prominent anchor tenant. Coincidentally, one of the other guests attending the meeting was a CEO of another well-known retailer. When the developer stated his intentions, the other guest (the retailer) told him that the anchor tenant of the mall across the street was going dark (real estate parlance for closing the store). He said the announcement was going to be forthcoming in the next couple of weeks. The suburban developer's complexion turned ashen. He was stunned. He had no idea the retailer would be leaving. His assumptions were based on the draw from that tenant. He aborted the deal. A few weeks later, the retailer announced the closing of the Westchester location. The guest was very thankful that he attended the meeting.

A recent guest was an entrepreneur in transition. This man built and sold a retail display manufacturing company. The noncompete clause in his contract had just expired, and he identified a company that he was negotiating to buy. The target company had problems and was poorly managed. He explained the transaction he was contemplating. The company sounded very familiar to me. It turns out that this company had approached my company (Mercury Capital) seeking financing. They were substantially behind in their real estate taxes and needed an infusion of cash. The collateral was their warehouse. The borrower represented a value, which was vastly overstated. In my business this is not an unusual occurrence. The warehouse was an esoteric property, an oddly shaped ten-story building. It was not a desirable warehouse site, and not easy to sell. (Generally, multilevel warehouses are not desirable for storage.)

Our guest assumed the value was what the company represented. When I told him the results of my due diligence, he paused. We met later in the day and went through the transaction thoroughly. I brought another member of the group to the meeting who is a turnaround expert. Our guest's assumptions were wrong. He was offering way too much money, and his strategy to acquire was flawed. We suggested a different approach, which entailed playing hardball. A number of months later our guest acquired the company for considerably less consideration.

> **Rule 25**
>
> Own your group like you own your business. Nourish it, and it will become an invaluable asset that will multiply your possibilities.

Being a good networker sometimes has its drawbacks. Occasionally, you will be wasting your time. I always tell people that my antennae are always extended for potential opportunities. I receive daily referrals. As a rule, I always qualify the opportunity prior to having a meeting. Once we had a guest at a cocktail party who was a highly regarded New York City official. Lou was a lovely guy and over time we became friends. Occasionally, Lou would call me with a business opportunity.

Last year, Lou asked me to meet with a good friend who had a great opportunity. I agreed. He promised me that I wouldn't be disappointed; I told Lou that I generally like to qualify the opportunity (in other words, do an informal reference check), but Lou insisted.

The next day, two weird-looking guys showed up in my office. They entered my conference room and placed a laptop on the table and started their presentation.

One man, let's call him Bob, began, "Mr. Meshel, we are about to show you something we have been working on for two years, and it's highly confidential. This could be like Häagen-Dazs ice cream. Can we count on you?" I knew instantly I was wasting my time. My instincts just told me that they were amateurs because their hyperbole was not to be believed.

I realized there was no escaping politely, so I said they could.

"Okay, imagine you have an aunt Bessie," says Bob. He turns on his laptop and depressing music is playing in the background. A video camera is touring a house, intermittently stopping to focus on paintings, urns, closets, the backyard, and so on. "Now suppose Aunt Bessie dies. When you go to the funeral parlor to arrange the burial you find you have a new option. For a nominal charge of $199 you can have Aunt Bessie stored in perpetuity on the Internet. We have invented the everlasting memorial. This is Aunt Bessie's house: her closets, her backyard, her slippers. We will store your aunt Bessie's memorial for you forever. Whenever you get the urge, you can go on your computer and retrieve the memorial."

I thought I had heard everything. I could barely keep from bursting out laughing. In fact, in retrospect, it could have been a satirical skit on *Saturday Night Live.* The presentation lasted forty-five minutes, and I was trying to figure out how I was going to gracefully get them out of my office.

"Isn't this incredible?" Bob concluded. "Everybody will buy it to remember his or her loved ones. We need $1.5 million to get this going. The funeral home market is huge."

"Guys," I said, "I've got to tell you that you both are geniuses. I am really impressed. Do you know the TV show *The Honeymooners*?"

They nodded.

"When that show was released, it didn't do well. Do you know why?"

I had to have some fun. They looked puzzled.

"*The Honeymooners,* when it was released, was way ahead of its time. The humor was great, but back in the fifties the show was considered risqué. Today, it's a winner. You guys suffer from the same ailment. The vision of your product is ahead of its time. I think as the Internet develops and people get used to storing their personal possessions digitally you will have a big success. Unfortunately, you're just too early." I kept my real thoughts to myself.

This was a small price to pay, of course, for being part of a networking group. Not every lead is going to be useful; not every referral is going to produce a multimillion-dollar payoff. Some people will walk into your office and their ideas will be beyond absurd. That's the way it is. Most important are traffic flow and the level of activity generated by the group. Actually, with heavy traffic coming your way, not every referral is going to be worthwhile. It's hit or miss. But meet with enough people and you're going to hit far more often than you miss. Or at least your successes will outweigh the cost of the time that you put into all those meetings that don't lead to anything worthwhile.

12

Networking Intelligence
Managing Your Business

I've always been uncomfortable with the pejorative connotations of networking which suggest accumulating new business contacts only for the self-serving purpose of making deals. There is so much more to it than that. An expanded definition includes another important aspect. I call it "networking intelligence," and it roughly means gaining knowledge to do your job better or operate your business more profitably and efficiently. Networking intelligence can be done informally, of course, among business contacts you already know; and many people do this already. But there are several organizations that specialize in this kind of networking. Business professionals periodically sit down in a conference room where they're comfortable with each other, and everything they discuss is confidential. They'll talk about how to deal with various issues and how to analyze in detail what's going on. Big issues, like how the world economy will affect their business, are also on the table. It's a think tank, if you will, of intelligence, knowledge, and insights. It's a powerful connection.

In this chapter, I'll sketch the highlights of three of the more prominent organizations: The Executive Committee (TEC), Young Presidents Organization (YPO), and World Presidents Organization (WPO).

THE EXECUTIVE COMMITTEE

Founded in 1957, TEC was the brainchild of a Wisconsin businessman who had lost a large contract with Montgomery Ward. When his lawn mower company went belly up as a result, he thought about organizing other executives who had experienced similar business crises. He didn't want to see others face the same fate he had. In the past half century, TEC has grown into a movement that is now embraced by more than nine thousand executives worldwide with four hundred chapters. Emerging entrepreneurs, chief executives, presidents, and owners of businesses compose its membership. Networking in this platform is about enhancing the business of its members. Most leaders are surrounded by people with agendas and sometimes rely on biased views (often subordinate senior executives who may be focused on advancing their own position within a company). Peer groups—namely, CEOs, presidents, and other heads of organizations—give each other an objective view and encourage greater accountability.

Each chapter has fourteen to sixteen members. No one in a group is in the same business, nor can a member in a group do business with another member in the same group. The prescription is for candor and confidentiality. The chair of the group creates an environment of implicit trust between the members. It is contingent upon the participants to bring up the real issues and opportunities regarding their businesses. A member must be willing to reveal his strategies, insights, and weaknesses.

A Columbia graduate started a tech business with two partners in the 1980s. He realized he had great instincts for business but no experience whatsoever as a CEO. His business was flourishing, but he had no idea if he was running the company well. He questioned whether he could do better. He grappled with the changing landscape and wondered how to take advantage of opportunities.

When he joined TEC, he found himself in a room with a Wharton School of Business graduate, a high school dropout, a guy who had graduated at the top of his class at MIT, and various other business owners. Eventually, the group helped him develop marketing strategies, set up an organizational structure, and develop both a leadership philosophy and a strategic plan.

As years went by, he brought the results to the group to be critiqued. Monthly issues consisting of finance, marketing, and personnel strategies were discussed and analyzed. The group inquired about what was accomplished in the past thirty days and quizzed him on his next thirty-day goals.

The larger issues were discussed, as well—how to expand into other markets and establish the firm as a preferred vendor to Fortune 500 companies. If he could achieve these results he would create enterprise value for the company.

In ten years' time, he sold the company to a public company for around $70 million, a multiple of eleven times earnings, when the current market was seven to eight times earnings. Much of his success was due to the rigorous analysis done by the TEC group.

THE S CURVE:
A COMMERCIAL WALL-COVERING COMPANY

A son, in his thirties, took over his father's wall-covering firm. Because he did not apprentice with his father, the son knew nothing about the business. The revenues, growth, and success data echoed the classic S curve that began when the father started the company after World War II. (The S curve of a company follows a life cycle where it grows, peaks, flattens, and then, inevitably declines. The longer the curve, the more successful the enterprise.) The father ran his business the old-fashioned way: He took all the money out during the years he ran the company. He didn't understand why his son couldn't duplicate his success after he retired. The father had left his son an antiquated company; the personnel had aged and not kept up with the times; the technology was legacy-based and not very useful. Meanwhile, the competitive environment had become fierce.

Growth had now stopped, and the son put significant issues on the back burner. Unless he recognized the dramatic change, the inevitability of the S curve would be that the business would rapidly decline. The Executive Committee showed him that if he did not act proactively over the next three years, he would gross $49 million with expenses of $48 million. The challenge: How could he reduce or contain his expenses and use his existing platform to double his business?

The group encouraged him to make personnel changes that he wouldn't have done. He learned to get really good people even if he had to overpay. The company became more structured and disciplined. It changed in ways his father never would have dreamed of. It adapted to modern times.

The business the son inherited effectively was a distributor of manufacturers' commercial wall coverings. The manufacturers he was distributing for were defining the future. The adjustment he made was that he devised a program of his own designs, which gave him proprietary products. The bulk of his business was still defined by the manufacturers. However, he created an identity in the marketplace that enabled his company to go from number seven to number two in gross sales in the industry. He began branding every sample. His logo became widely recognized, and his company is now regarded as a formidable competitor once again.

THE YOUNG PRESIDENTS ORGANIZATION

In 1944, after serving in the U.S. Army during World War II, Ray Hickock returned home and joined his father's company, Hickock Belts. Shortly thereafter, his father passed away. A year later, the company's board voted for Ray Hickock to become president and CEO at twenty-eight. Hickok knew that he had limited experience and was insecure about his judgment. At that time, the U.S. business community included few young executives with major responsibilities. He faced unusual problems and began meeting with other CEOs who faced similar issues. So he conceived the idea of a membership organization for young CEOs.

When Ray Hickock opened the first meeting of the Young Presidents Organization in 1950, not even he realized the impact it would have on the world of business. By sharing their experiences, those first twenty young presidents helped one another cope with the unusual pressures and pleasures of early success. Hickock's brilliantly simple concept has proven to be what the business world needed for many executives and company owners. The YPO now has a worldwide membership approaching eleven thousand. (Certain specific financial and personnel thresholds must be attained by the company for the CEO to qualify for membership). In addition, you have to be under forty-four years old. Consequently, the membership requirements of the YPO attract many second- and third-generation family businesses.

I've interviewed many members, and, in every case, they say that the YPO has been beneficial to both their business and personal lives.

Currently, the YPO has 160 chapters worldwide, while the Metro New York chapter has 250 members. In each chapter, a member has the opportunity to break out into smaller groups and meet monthly. These individual groups are called forums. Each forum consists of ten members who are in different businesses and are not doing business with each other. All the members are presidents of their companies and generally have strong convictions and opinions.

"Losers, Cruisers, and Doers"

One YPO member said to me that the world consists of three types of individuals: losers, cruisers, and doers. Losers are pessimists and inept at almost everything they try. Losers don't want to change, and they don't want to learn because it involves a lot of work. Cruisers can go either way. A cruiser can become a loser or a doer depending on the motivational skills that they learn. Doers just get it done. They are leaders. YPOers tend to be doers.

The forum is an environment where the participants deal with the same challenges in business and share different perspectives. Their advice is substantive. You learn methods and techniques that you may never have considered. In these meetings, no one has to apologize for their strength of character. Everybody is similar.

There is actually a specific training program given by the YPO that instructs members in decorum and proper forum participation. It is mandatory to learn and abide by the forum protocol. One member showed me a card he carries that has listed on it the protocol rules:

1. Be specific.
2. Use "I" statements.
3. Speak from experience.
4. Share something of myself before asking a question.
5. No interrogation.

6. No "fix its," no "you shoulds," and no advice.

7. Share information, opinions, and experiences with my forum members.

There is a science behind these aphorisms. Ego and strong opinions need to be moderated, and suggestions must be constructive.

The forum protocol teaches how to articulate in the YPO way. The rules are stringent. If a member misses more than two forum meetings in a year he is ousted. Each member must go through the formal training. One member I interviewed moderates several forums. Rob sold his company and currently is an entrepreneur in transition. Rob realized that he wasn't unique and that there were many YPOers that sold their companies or retired or were otherwise in limbo. In his chapter, Rob started a theme forum, positioned for YPOers who are in a state of transition. The issues are different, but the conversation and suggestions are equally candid and erudite.

Forums have been known to stay together for thirty to forty years. Great friendships are developed and the support is familial.

Back to School

As I've mentioned earlier, a thirst for knowledge will help keep you ahead of the curve. Learning on a formal basis can be beneficial at any time during your career. I was reading a story about one YPOer who attended a Hong Kong university. He ran a toy distribution business and felt that he had adequately kept up with technology until he went back to school. He then realized that he knew virtually nothing about e-commerce; his company was in the dark ages when it came to the Internet. He returned home and implemented an online strategy that lever-

aged his business. Today, he admits that he would not have implemented the e-commerce business nearly as well if he hadn't
attended the Hong Kong school.

The "university" phase of the YPO takes place all over the
world. Members get to meet world leaders and share insights they
never would have if it weren't for being part of the organization.

Taking Inventory of Your Skills

The value of networking is most powerfully illustrated by another facet of the YPO called the Inventory of Skills Foundation,
or IOS. The foundation maintains a database about the special
skills of YPO members, and members of other organizations,
that enables YPOers to tap in and locate resources to help with
business or personal problems, consult on medical issues or dis-
abilities, or provide information on a variety of other challenges.
The information for the database is collected via a confidential
questionnaire, usually distributed by the membership chairman
or during a chapter meeting, at workshops, or other YPO events.
Some twelve hundred issues are covered on this enrollment form.

In addition, the IOS looks for third-party references to provide additional information and recommendations. For example,
U.S. News & World Report is a reference that provides indepen-
dent ratings on the top hospitals in the country. The IOS integrates
this information into the database to cross-reference membership submissions and provide additional information from outside sources.

There are two kinds of referral services offered by IOS. One
is for medical requests, doctor to membership information, for
example; the other is a referral service that includes any area of
your life where you would like a member's help and guidance.
This includes advice on family, finance, business, education issues, and even vacations.

How does it work? The process begins with a telephone call to IOS. Once you've told them what you are looking for, they send a blind inquiry to the YPO members who indicated in the enrollment questionnaire that they have expertise in that area. It's a no-obligation, no-hurt feelings help desk, so to speak. The recipients of the blind inquiry can respond or not. No one, except for the administrator at IOS, knows who received the inquiry. This system was established and is maintained with the highest regard for each member's privacy.

YPO has compiled testimonies from members extolling how the organization has benefited them. One member mentioned seven members talking with Bill Gates for four hours at a Las Vegas meeting. He said the opportunity came directly from being part of the YPO. Another member lauded his coforum members, who convinced him to leave a CEO position to join another company that ultimately went public. Whoever you are, whatever you are doing, YPO membership allows you to get close to other CEOs in a private and exclusive environment, enabling you to learn more about the opportunities that are out there. A significant percentage of the testimonies thanked the IOS for introductions that made a difference.

YPO has other resources as well. Rob, a friend of mine, told me when his mother had a stroke, he reached out to the YPO for help. The head of the department of the Princeton Stroke Unit called him. The contacts he was introduced to were at the highest of levels and really made a difference in her care.

WORLD PRESIDENTS ORGANIZATION

A former YPO member summed up his experience: "Soon after joining, I began to experience self-doubts. I was faced with questions I had not fully contemplated in the past. My life was not in balance, and there was a lot to learn. What a challenge. I had a good business, but everyone else seemed to have bigger and better businesses. I had traveled the globe, but everyone else was coming or going. I had great family values, and everyone was searching to reach higher levels. That was my strength. There was commonality and division. I felt encouraged at times and discouraged at other times. I loved it and I hated it. That was ten years ago. Wow! What a great ride! I learned, I contributed, and I came out winning. These experiences cannot be gained anywhere. Now at forty-nine, I dread the end."

At the age of forty-nine, a YPO member is required to graduate from the organization. (The ritual includes a party where the graduating YPO member receives a rocking chair.) Fortunately, the graduating YPO member has the opportunity to enroll into the World Presidents Organization (WPO). Only retiring YPOers are eligible to become members.

The WPO has more than 3,850 business people who are or have been chief executive officers of major business enterprises. With operations in more than sixty countries, WPO members combine corporate responsibility and personal public service to create significant contributions in the communities where they live and work. Today, their ranks include diplomats and senior elected and appointed government officials on international, national, regional, and local levels. As lifetime leaders, WPO members recognize and act on their responsibility in the fields of corporate governance, public service, and educational advancement.

As a YPO graduate organization, the WPO offers its members an advanced level of serious but stimulating educational programming and simultaneously draws from the wealth of talent and achievement within its own ranks.

Formed originally as the World Business Council by 176 graduates of YPO, the group expanded rapidly in 1991 and changed its name to the World Presidents Organization to reflect its growth, not just in membership but also in global reach. At around the same time, WPO strengthened its impetus for more formalized local activities. Within five years, nearly forty chapters had been formed. Today, there are more than sixty-five chapters worldwide.

At every level—local, regional, national, and international—WPO is dedicated to the mission it shares with YPO: "Building better presidents through education, idea exchange, and networking." This mission is an articulation of the organization's intense focus on the candid exchange of ideas. Dedicated to freedom of expression beyond what might normally be possible in settings sponsored by corporate or government entities, WPO takes no political or ideological position.

Educational Programs and Events

The WPO annually sponsors a variety of educational programs. The largest among these programs are held at universities—weeklong sessions that feature a faculty of political and economic leaders, scientists and educators, artists and writers, and corporate and academic experts. To enhance the formal lectures, university programs include offsite meetings designed to provide firsthand business and cultural experience in the host country. Seminars and targeted activity groups are smaller programs that give members with special intellectual or professional interests the opportunity to learn from each other as well as from experts in fields such as financial management, science, history, public affairs, international relations, health, and business or personal development.

On the regional and local levels, conferences and chapter meetings provide additional opportunities for idea exchange. Perennially, a highly valued offering is the President's Forum through which a group of ten to twenty individuals meet regularly to hone their professional and personal skills in a confidential setting. Unique to WPO is the Global Forum, drawing members from different nationalities to broaden cultural understanding and strengthen ties across political and social boundaries.

Whether the meetings are large or small, the scope worldwide or narrowly focused, WPO educational formats recognize the intellectual curiosity, leadership, and keen understanding of the members. At the same time, WPO policy specifies that spouses be included in meetings, and members are periodically encouraged to include adult offspring. With the involvement of the full spectrum of member families and the interfaces on the exchange of ideas, WPO programs offer unique, usable insights members cannot find elsewhere.

The main difference between the WPO and the YPO is that the WPO concentrates on issues that are more germane to older businessmen and -women. Personal problems take on more urgency than some immediate business questions. For example, WPO's Forum groups, which meet once a month, and have a dozen or so attendees, may look at things like divorce, real estate, insurance, succession in family-run businesses, and so on. "It's a very effective global network," said one member. "I have people in the WPO I've been friendly with for more than thirty years. At last night's Forum meeting, two people announced career changes, and the group was there to support them."

13

Raising the Bar
The Network Advantage

A pessimist sees the difficulty in every opportunity.
An optimist sees the opportunity in every difficulty.
—*Winston Churchill*

Once you've achieved a fair amount of fluency, comfort, and success within a networking group, you should be able to formulate new outside opportunities with just a little extra effort. The best networkers are adept at creating their own platforms. They are constantly thinking about the next contact in venues that others might not consider. Where will I find my next deal or my next sale? A brief list of possibilities:

➤ Philanthropy. Have you joined any committees or boards involving a charity that you are partial to? There is a direct correlation between successful businesspeople and individuals who are members of philanthropic or service-oriented boards.

➤ Schools. Are you a member of the PTA or on the board of your children's school? Most have an eclectic mix of people, and it is inevitable that you will eventually meet someone in your business orbit.

➤ Village or town government. If you live in a small village
  or town, have you considered volunteering for a civic
  cause? Is there a business improvement society or a cham-
  ber of commerce where you can offer your expertise? The
  Little League, the library?

➤ A cause of any kind. Sometimes opportunities abound in
  what may first appear to be mundane issues: expanding
  the local library, opening a reading room for children, sav-
  ing a wetland, or preserving open wilderness space.

I have used these types of resources to my advantage over a
period of several years. Today, I am on four different boards
(some are corporate). Each one is a different platform with various members. I have cultivated relationships that have led to all
sorts of opportunities. There are many types of platforms; if
you make an effort to build your own, I guarantee it will reap
dividends.

The key to the new platform has to include your asking and
answering the following critical question: "How can I stand out?"
You must differentiate yourself from your competitors, your colleagues, and your peers, who may lack insight and imagination.
When you're able to do that, you'll be considered an omniscient
source. Have your sensors up in order to get ready to stand out.

THE MAYOR OF THE EXECUTIVE LOCKER ROOM

You can create a new networking platform almost anywhere. I
even used my local gym's locker room. For several years, I've
been a member of the LA Sports Club in New York. I joined primarily because I believe in staying in shape. But I also recognized that there could be business opportunities waiting in the
lounge. The club offers two types of membership: a regular mem-

bership at $1,300 a year and an executive membership at $2,600 a year. The difference between memberships is that the executive option includes additional club amenities and the use of all the club's locations. In the executive locker room, members get permanent lockers, and their workout clothes are always freshly laundered. The lounge has couches and a flat-screen television. Each morning, attendants provide orange juice and fresh fruit at no charge.

I joined the club during the initial campaign to draft members one year prior to the opening. At that time, the club's salesperson promised many amenities that had not been provided when the club opened, such as eucalyptus in the steam room. We got the steam room but no eucalyptus.

One day, the club summarily did away with the free orange juice. When asked why, management claimed that members were filling their water bottles with the orange juice and taking the bottles home. Besides being insulting, the excuse was ridiculous. Can you imagine flying first-class and the stewardess telling you the airline has stopped serving food because passengers were stuffing the caviar into their purses? It was obvious that the club wasn't doing as well as it hoped, and it was beginning to cut back.

In the regular locker room, there is a full-time attendant for the members. In the executive locker room, there was never anybody around. Every time we needed something, we had to call the front desk, and ten minutes later an attendant would appear. The executive members complained, but nothing changed.

One day, I was working out with Joe, also an executive member. Joe was really annoyed about the lack of service and was considering leaving the club.

I smelled an insurrection. And when I smell an insurrection, I sense an opportunity. I told Joe to stay tuned, especially to the locker room walls. I decided to rally the troops by filing a petition.

I wrote a complaint letter, and I began posting it around the

Rule 26 Create an opportunity by solving a problem, taking advantage of the platform, and planning a strategy that makes you a magnet.

locker area. One member read it and immediately approached me. "Hey, Jeff," he said. "This is great. You're right. Here is my number and e-mail address. I'm 100 percent behind you." At least twenty others approached and promised full support. One member asked me if I was a lawyer. I told him no, just a concerned activist, and I briefly explained my business. It wasn't long before I effectively became the mayor of the locker room.

After I finished taping up all of my letters, I went downstairs to work out. I wasn't in the gym for more than fifteen minutes when a club employee asked me to the office. I ended up having a very tense conversation with Karen, the club's manager. I listed all the things we were promised when we joined, the amenities that were revoked, and all the items that weren't in working order.

She said she would get back to me. A week or so later, I received a letter from management stating that I violated the bylaws of the club. The letter said something like "soliciting" on the club premises was prohibited. It was a lame and ludicrous ploy to persuade me to desist from getting the members to make a mass protest.

Now, I was really steamed. When I called Karen to get an explanation, she assured me that her response wasn't a threat and that the executive membership would see results immediately.

The following week, a big laminated sign on an easel was placed at the door of the executive locker room. It read: "We Hear You!" It listed all the amenities that were going to be added to the executive locker room with a timetable. Eventually, we got what we paid for—and demanded.

Why did I volunteer to champion this cause?

It was a great opportunity to meet other executive members without directly promoting my own agenda. There is an interesting psychology in the executive locker room. Everybody is naturally curious about what the guy drying himself off next to him does for a living. When someone started a conversation with another executive member, he always got to the key question, so what do you do? This curiosity stems from the assumption that if you're an executive member, you probably are successful in business.

And I really wanted my eucalyptus in the steam room.

As of this writing, I've developed at least six pieces of business that originated in the executive locker room. What I eventually earned from these transactions was far in excess of the cost of being a member.

> **Rule 27**
>
> If you can afford it, fly first class. You never know who will be sitting next to you.

TIGER 21—THE INVESTOR GROUP FOR ENHANCED RESULTS

Six years ago, Michael Sonnenfeldt had an interesting problem. An accomplished businessman who sold his real estate firm in the late 1990s, he woke up one morning and realized he had been a very successful businessman but that he really knew very little about investing the wealth he had created. The isolation of leadership was now replaced by the loneliness of wealth (though most would argue that if you had to be lonely, you might as well have the tens of millions Sonnenfeldt had). As a businessman, he found himself up at 3:00 A.M. agonizing over his issues, knowing that everyone else was sleeping. Now that he was wealthy, the issues were different, but the responsibility seemed just as important. *He realized he didn't even know what he didn't know.* The skill set that he had developed to build a business was not necessarily the one that would help him preserve or enhance his wealth as a passive investor in other companies or financial instruments.

Most people with newfound wealth are counseled that a prudent approach is to assemble a diversified portfolio, in which any specific investment loss would not be devastating. Sonnenfeldt believed that if he could have created such a portfolio that spread the risks, minimized the potential for loss, and was likely to provide what he deemed was a reasonable amount of income, he would have gladly turned over the portfolio to trusted advisers. But the investment environment was changing so rapidly, and the risks from tech bubbles, terrorism, and the impact of globalism on the dollar and the U.S. economy's supremacy were growing rapidly. He felt it would be irresponsible to cede control to advisers who often lacked perspective on matters beyond their specific expertise, who were blind to certain risks they were exposing their clients to. Often these advisers had little to lose by giving bad advice, and, even more often, they seemed to profit from fees whether their clients made or lost money. Financial advisers, fund managers, bankers, family members, well-intentioned friends, and others, all proffering expertise, frequently had an agenda. Too often, they wanted to sell him something or manage his money for fees that would cloud their judgment.

Sonnenfeldt thought that there might be others like himself who were facing similar issues and needed to address the anxieties and realities of significant net worth.

So Sonnenfeldt assembled a group of his well-heeled friends and associates and started Tiger 21, which *Fortune* magazine called "part investment club, part group therapy." Basically, the group has day-long private gatherings where members make presentations of their personal portfolios. A member has to be willing to reveal all of his assets to the other members—within the private and confidential setting of the monthly group meeting. The presenting member discloses his investments in precise detail, and when he's finished, the group barrages him with questions. He has to mount a logical defense of where he puts his money. The portfolio defense is like a cross-examination, but the club members prefer to call it "care-frontational." After all, there's no gain in insulting or agitating a fellow member with an eight-figure net worth.

Tiger 21 members meet once a month to help each other become more effective investors and money managers. The organization requires a net worth of between $10 million and $100 million.

The monthly meeting allows these members to create an empathetic environment where they can candidly discuss their issues and opportunities. The group is professionally facilitated and operates on the principle that they are there to *help* each other, not *judge* each other. In addition to the discussion around member issues, the members invite investment advisers, fund managers, bankers, and other investment service providers to make presentations and answer questions. After a presentation, the group can confidentially and dispassionately discuss the viability of an investment opportunity and/or for whom it might be appropriate among the members. The group also invites professionals to educate them about investment strategies, lawyers to tell them about tax and wealth transfer issues, economists to project trends, and futurists to help them look over the horizon. In addition to having successful and smart business people evaluate the allocation of the assets, the group has created a platform that attracts investment opportunities.

A group like Tiger 21 expands the breadth of the definition of networking.

ELECTRONIC NETWORKS—IS THIS THE FUTURE?

In the past few years, a number of Web sites have been developed to accommodate those who want to network online. In fact, David Teten, who wrote a book about electronic networking, estimates there are some two hundred sites that provide introductions among members. They are all trying to differentiate themselves in providing specific services, but the field is very crowded and expected to thin quickly. There are just so many competitors that the market can accommodate, and the weaker ones will eventually drop out. Teten is associated with Online Business Networks, whose mandate is "building quality business relationships online." Teten said, "We've grown very rapidly. I think we now have over seven hundred thousand people mixers."

Two of the more popular networking sites are Orkut and Linkedin. Orkut appears to be directed more toward social relationships, while Linkedin is unabashedly aimed at business professionals looking to expand their contact list. Spoke is another such site, and it targets enterprise sales forces. Its business model is not unlike Microsoft's, in that it sells its software on a "perseat" basis to other companies.

Linkedin is probably the best-known site at this time. You can't just join Linkedin; you must be asked to join by a current member. Then you submit a short biography, and you can then browse the membership database, which is accessed in several ways. The software that runs Linkedin delineates each member's closeness to other members. For example, it will list your "direct connections," which include "close friends and colleagues." Then it will list others who are "two degrees, three degrees, and four degrees" away. Finally, it will tell you how many people you have access to "through a trusted referral."

A first contact is always made indirectly and by consent of

the party being solicited. The referral system is discreet, private, and secure, according to those familiar with the site. If you see a contact name whom you'd like to meet, you can then send an e-mail to someone he or she is connected with, who will then attempt an introduction. At the time of this writing, Linkedin had not yet begun charging members for their initial requests for contacts. (It does ask you to fill out a questionnaire seeking to find out what services you'll pay for, and how much you're willing to pay.) It appears that the economic model is still being worked on. But the idea has potential, and the site claims several thousand members.

Is electronic networking a good idea? Will the sites catch on? These are excellent questions, and nobody can answer them conclusively at this time.

It is likely that these Web sites can be an additional tool for those who already are excellent networkers. They will not make shy people become extroverted. But at this point, I do believe that networking is primarily a face-to-face activity. This is why we still get on airplanes and fly halfway around the world to meet with potential customers and cement relationships with our best clients. Any technology that dilutes this experience undermines the basic networking tenets.

At this point in their history, I have strong reservations about using these Web sites, especially exclusive of physical-meeting networks. Currently, the electronic networks have to fight the perception that there are security and privacy risks. Granted, the risks may be minimal, but they exist. Could an expert hacker delve into my database, or Linkedin's computers? Probably one could, however unlikely the possibility. More specifically, what about spammers? Despite the best efforts of the software designers, it makes me shudder with fear that the four thousand people in my electronic address book could be the recipients of endless e-mails promising larger body parts or endless riches from African potentates. David Teten said Spoke has hired a chief privacy officer with a very strong background in managing this kind of risk. In general, there are certain steps you can take to minimize your risk, but then I'm just not sure how much of a hassle people will tolerate to develop online contacts.

Despite these caveats, I'm still a great believer that the Internet will continue to facilitate conventional business activity. Now that it's been in common use for a decade or more, I often wonder how the world got along without it.

14

How Other Experts Network
Three Points of View

Nothing is absolute, of course, especially in the world of networking. What works for one person may not work for another. There are a lot of different ways to form relationships and connections, and everyone has his or her own way of doing it. I've picked three businessmen with different points of view to explain how they go about networking. Not only do these three men have distinct approaches but also their philosophies are not always attuned to my own. I'm going to let them talk about their methods directly, in their own words.

Jeff Bauman, the principal of Network Sales Consulting, is a talent in the business services sector. His universe is very different from mine in that his sale is made at a different level of the corporate hierarchy. Jeff has mastered finding specific service providers that meet his criteria. He commingles them, overlaps them, and approaches customers with multiple service skill sets. This team of providers becomes a one-step solution. If you sell a business service, you could learn a lot by his methodology.

Bauman is very direct when trying to sell you, whereas I'm not. Bauman's goal when he meets a potential client is to identify an area that he can impact in a positive way. Since most of the products he sells are commodities, it is important for him to establish a level of credibility that separates him as a person who delivers added value. I take the long view and let you see what I do. I have a more subtle way of approaching people. But he's selling a different type of product. And it works for him.

Jeff's a blender. He's always mixing and matching. He is in four different networking groups, and he's constantly gathering all these people together with the hope that it generates opportunities.

Networking is a natural extension of my personality. I like meeting new people. If this doesn't sound appealing, you probably will never be a good networker. In the past thirty-five years, I have met thousands of people. There's no way every one of them could be actively involved in a relationship with me. However, I immediately make an assessment. Even if they do not have a direct connection with my primary business, I am more interested in their commitment to establishing a relationship and possibly joining my team.

What do I mean by my team? Basically, the people who are networking at the same level of commitment as I am. Their understanding of networking is aligned with mine. They unconditionally participate in supporting another team member's request and deliver results based on years of relationships. Identifying these people is one of the key elements in determining your success. It is not unlike a coach assessing talent for his team.

Recently I was asked to help a telecommunications consultant find a way to get in front of more decision makers at a time when they would be more energized to make a decision. I recognized a very important condition in the market that could benefit a company in an audit. These audits, for even midsized companies, could yield six- and seven-figure refunds based on the fact that they could go back six years. (The important condition is that a company must still be operating out of the space where the phone lines were installed.)

It was obvious to me that people who are dependent on the event of a company moving could offer a phenomenal gift to any client or prospective client that is in the process of—or considering—making a move. Real estate brokers, architects, those in the moving business, all became potential leads for my telecommunications consultant, since this introduction would only enhance their status with their client or prospect. I set up meetings with people from each of these fields and was excited to see their positive reactions. They immediately recognized the additional value proposition that was created by this introduction. A win for all. The telecom consultant gained access to people who were in a decision-making position. The brokers, architects, and movers created a financial windfall opportunity for their clients and additional credibility for themselves. The clients not only reaped a financial gain that they might not have been aware of but they also gained a new perspective on the person who initiated the opportunity. That person was I.

When I established my business, Network Sales Consulting, the idea was to assist companies in developing business strategies that could achieve measurable results. Networking principles are universal across all vertical markets; my assignments have varied commensurately. Yet it is the relationships I have developed that have given me the experience to create alternative go-to market strategies and the firepower to achieve the results that my clients are looking for.

By listening to my clients' presentation of their products and services and asking challenging questions, I usually discover new opportunities and possibilities that were previously not part of the initial business plan.

COMMON DENOMINATORS

One way to shortcut the time I spend pursuing the appropriate contact at a target customer is to identify the most appropriate people who are already in an existing relationship with them. I call these common denominators. My target customers were facilities managers in charge of regional retail centers. I did not want to pursue each relationship on an individual basis. In searching for a common denominator, I recalled the responses I had received from people in executive positions for retail chains. Mostly, they wanted to reduce expenses and create new efficiencies. In my quest to find a solution that could separate my client from his competition, I decided to look for a technology product with specific attributes that could support facilities managers in charge of multiple locations. I identified a platform that became the hub of my wheel, another common denominator, if you will. I gave the facilities manager or property manager a one-stop solution to facilitate and manage all their subcontractors and expenses attached to those services.

A couple of months later, a gentleman appeared at a network meeting who had a technology product that supported retailers on their supply requirements. Immediately, I recognized the synergy between the two platforms and how, by bringing them together, I could achieve phenomenal results. I invited both companies to a meeting and within minutes both of them recognized the value of my idea. Between both platforms, we could provide retailers with aggregated information and services that would allow them to control all indirect expenses by looking at a one-system solution. To confirm our beliefs, I invited a consulting company in the retail industry to see a demonstration of the two products (knowing that these platforms would enhance their offering). Their reaction was consistent to ours. They realized that these two platforms combined could create baselines through the data collection that would achieve a higher plateau in controlling costs and managing services.

This illustrates how networking can really work.

How do I identify all the characteristics that I look for in a person that I will network with? Integrity and credibility are directly connected, and they are extremely important. I have a visceral sense of connecting people that bring value to each other. Win-win is a key goal when you bring people together. Once people in your networking circle know this, it becomes a win-win for you.

CONNECTING THE DOTS, ALL DAY, EVERY DAY

People you are networking with should never be prejudged based on their occupation or any other personal attribute. You never know whose relative, friend, child's friend, coworker, client, board member, or any other connection can be the difference in getting you in front of the right person.

Companies from both unrelated as well as synergistic industries can be connected to make business happen. The possibility is always there if people are open and willing to extend themselves. You must constantly recognize the value of a relationship that would enhance your client's business, even if it doesn't immediately enhance yours.

Choose your networking partners wisely. They will author your future success.

John E. Oden is a principal at Bernstein Investment Research Management, a money management and research firm (part of Alliance Capital). He and I are as different as day and night in many ways. But at the end of the day, we're also very similar in a lot of respects. He comes across as very confident—some of those who know him would call him overconfident to the point of arrogance. His philosophy is, "It's not who you know, rather, it's how few people you have to know." It's a different approach. I think he limits his opportunities. But it works well for him, and his methodology might prove to be attractive to you, too. John is a phenomenal networker. He is a very sharp guy and he always presents himself as someone you want to know. He is a guy who puts himself on center stage, right in the spotlight. He understands the concept of thinking big. While some networkers are deciding whether to attend a charity event, Oden is the first one to think, "Just buy the table and bring others."

As Jeff has told you, we've agreed to disagree on the best way to network. "It's not *who* you know, it's how *few* you *have* to know." I absolutely believe in this concept and when executed properly it can be the most effective way to operate.

How many times have you seen someone accomplish in a single phone call what some people cannot complete in days? I'm sure you've heard of someone who can set up a meeting with just the right person at IBM so he or she can make a sale? How does someone have that kind of power, that kind of clout? How does someone know who to call at GE Capital to immediately open the right door to create a merger or obtain financial backing? Or how does someone raise $100,000 for an investment opportunity from a top executive at Microsoft, or $25,000 for a charity from a Citigroup official, by placing just one phone call? There are people who can do these things.

I like the expressions "thread the needle," "hit the bull's-eye," "put a round peg in a round hole," and "go right to the jugular." These phrases imply that someone can sift through the clutter and get the job done quickly—not by knowing everyone but by knowing the right place to go at the right time.

How do you achieve this vision, this power? And do you

have to get to know everyone first in order to know just where to go to achieve the desired result? Is it possible to focus on the few who can really help you, rather than the multitudes you meet along the way? Do you walk away from a cocktail party with twenty business cards, or one or two really good ones? Finally, how do you pick out the one or two really good ones? The answer to some of these questions is often not readily obvious.

Rule 28
Think big!!

Throughout my entire career, I have been in the business of raising money. From 1983 to 1992, I was an investment banker with a real estate orientation. As director of institutional placement (for real estate) at Drexel Burnham Lambert (now defunct) and as a managing director and national director of institutional accounts at Cushman & Wakefield, I raised more than $3 billion from institutions for real estate deals. Since then, as a principal of Bernstein, I have focused on raising money from private sources and have raised well over $1 billion over the past ten years. In my position at Bernstein, I focus on private companies, family offices, wealthy individuals, trusts, estates, foundations, and endowments. There is a plethora of people and companies in the money-raising business. How does someone achieve success in the highly competitive business of raising money?

In my business, the business of money management, it takes just as much time to work with a small client as with a large client. Small clients can be just as demanding and think they have just as much of a right to my time and attention as large clients. Time is everything. Develop a strategy that allows you to tap into larger relationships. I get a lot of my business from accountants, attorneys, and consultants. I try to determine which of these firms has the larger clients and then successfully position myself and our company to be on these firms' short list of prospective managers. As a result, I have developed some very large clients. Further, I am constantly weeding out smaller clients by transferring them to younger members of the firm who appreciate the business and have more time to spend with them.

This is equally true in the institutional arena. When I was raising money for big real estate projects, I always went first to the big players—Prudential, Equitable, Aetna, New York Life, Travelers, and Metropolitan Life. GE Capital was a great source for almost anything. These companies were consistently in the business, either as a buyer or a seller. I did hundreds of millions of dollars with these few players. At Drexel, we had an expression—"get in their face." I was in the faces of these companies constantly.

Rule
29

Less is more—constantly weed people out of your database.

I am a firm believer in the Eighty-Twenty rule—you get 80 percent of your business from 20 percent of your clients. When raising money from institutions, it is easy to know who the 80 percent are; however, this is not the case when dealing with individuals. Therefore, this can be a very painstaking and disciplined process. In working with large institutions, I keep almost everyone's business card because people move around in large organizations, and you never know who might be able to help you. However, with individuals, there are many people who will add little significant value to you in the long run. I prefer to eliminate them as soon as possible from my database so that I can focus on those people who are most likely to help me expand my circle of influence. When it comes to individuals, it is very easy to meet a lot of people and have them bog down your database. I would rather concentrate on a smaller number of people with whom I feel I can develop a mutually beneficial relationship. This way, when I place a phone call, call in a favor, or try to get something done with someone on my database, I can be reasonably assured that they know me and will respond.

Rule 30 To the extent you can, merge your business life with your personal life.

I live in New York City, which is a cultural haven. There are a lot of people in New York whose professions are involved in music, the arts, and the theater, and a lot of wealth created by those who are successful in these fields. I personally enjoy many of these endeavors and wondered how I might capitalize on this in business. So shortly after I joined Bernstein in 1992, I decided to actively pursue the media/entertainment industry. Over the course of several years, I used our firm's research analysts to give conferences specifically targeted at the media/entertainment business, where an overview of various segments of the business was reviewed and discussed, such as the television networks, Hollywood, Broadway, the music business, et cetera. These conferences were very well received, and I later formed an organization of professional advisers who specialize in the industry, which led to more contacts in the business and even more clients.

In addition, I also get exposure to the media/entertainment business through my philanthropic and cultural activities. For example, I am on the board of New Dramatists, a powerful fifty-

year-old organization that helps young playwrights and is supported by many movie stars and show business personalities.
We have a luncheon every year, and I always host a table. I have
had Lou Diamond Phillips, Lauren Bacall, Eli Wallach, Brian
Dennehy, Bernadette Peters, and Sigourney Weaver at my table.
Also, through my involvement with Carnegie Hall, the Metropolitan Opera Club, the Manhattan School of Music, and other
organizations, I have successfully melded what I do in the day-
time with the activities I love in my spare time.

> **Rule 31**
>
> Be passionate about something, and become an expert in something.

I read somewhere that the ancient Greeks did not write an
obituary about a man when he died; they just asked if he had
passion. I think that passion is what can separate a great person
from an exceptional person, a great idea from an extraordinary
idea. Passion is what makes something or someone be all that
they can become. How many times have you asked someone how
they are and they say, "Oh, same ole, same ole"? I cannot stand
people who think like that. For me, every day is an adventure, and
I wake up every morning looking forward to taking on the world.

Being passionate about something is one thing—being an
expert is quite another. Expertise is more grueling than passion—
it is the nuts and bolts of passion. It is "proving" passion or turning it into something more practical.

> **Rule 32**
>
> Use your time efficiently. Be nice to everyone but available to few.

It should be noted that my remarks are directed toward internal communication—not communication with clients. One must always be readily available to one's clients. They are the lifeblood of any organization.

Time is at the top of my list of precious commodities. There are a number of things that I feel strongly about in this regard. For example, I simply cannot stand it when people come into my office and want to talk about what happened in football over the weekend. This is not just because I don't care that much for football; it just takes too much time. People in my firm have sometimes described me as unapproachable. That's actually not true. I am approachable, but not for idle chatter. People know they can come to me with an important question. They know to stay away if they want to talk about how the Mets did on Saturday afternoon.

I look at the time all day long. I am constantly fighting the clock. I keep a clock in the office turned away from me, so people who are meeting me can see how much of *my* time they are taking. I am always looking to make one more call, to look over one more project, to write one more letter. The extra effort can make the difference.

Organization is the key to survival in the business world. It is the key to time management. Every weekend, I completely organize myself for the coming week. When I arrive on Monday morning, I am already in overdrive. I have an agenda and I am ready to go. My business depends on my initiating the action. My job is to make things happen. Delegation is the key to efficiency. I delegate everything I possibly can. It helps me get the job done and helps those who report to me learn the job.

I never use the word "try" and will challenge anyone who uses it to me. What does the word "try" mean exactly? It is nothing but a cop-out by the person who uses it—giving *them* the option to not perform on a certain task. When I ask for something and the response is "I'll try," I immediately challenge them to explain what they meant by that answer. My business is such that I need commitments from people and, in turn, I commit to my clients. I am demanding but I do not ask the impossible of those I work with. I would rather hear "It'll be tough, but we'll manage somehow" or "How about if you assign two people to work with me on this, to make sure it gets done?" Or "I simply cannot do this unless I can get help." With this information, I can work with them to make things happen and ensure that I am not going to walk in the next morning and be disappointed because someone tried but did not perform at my expense.

People think of "closing" a deal as some big, monumental event. It is actually a series of smaller events. However, any one of the small events, if not handled properly and professionally,

> Rule 33
>
> Closing is not a big event, rather a series of smaller ones.

can derail a closing. Our vice chairman, Roger Hertog, once told me, "Everyone makes great presentations. But everyone is *expected* to make great presentations. It's about being able to answer the tough questions after the presentation is over."

There is a lot of wisdom in this. Key questions answered decisively and authoritatively at just the right moment can lead straight to the closing.

How do you gain the attention of the president of General Motors, or the president of the Union Club, or the president of New York University if you are fortunate enough to meet them? You do so by performing whatever task you are asked to perform with great professionalism and style. You follow up, you engage them, and you find some way to establish a bond. You find some way to "get your nose under the tent." Then, you continue to move it forward. There is no set pattern, and it is easier said than done. You call on all of your firm's resources and all of your personal resources in order to accomplish this. You must be relentless but in a professional and intelligent way. You close on that person.

> **David Gensler,** the president of Madison Pension, is the poster boy for how to become a better networker. When I first met him, he had very little in the way of networking skills. When he realized how much he was lacking, he began to transform himself into someone who could be relatively at ease in a business or social situation. He has worked very diligently in the past five years to develop new contacts, and, at the same time, he has changed his business model. He went from an actuary to someone who manages large pension funds, and today he is much more successful on every level. His whole life has changed. Whereas he was once office bound and happy, he is now his firm's rainmaker. If you ask him, he will point out that he's constantly striving to be a better networker. He is a work in progress.

When my firm was formed in 1978, I was the classic "Mr. Inside." My responsibilities were technical. Accountants and other people in the financial services field directed business into our firm. In many cases (and I am not proud to admit this), I never met the client. Actually, in many cases, I never even *spoke* to the client. The business grew. Before long, we had a staff of more than twenty and our annual revenue was $3 million. I could do what I enjoyed and avoid what I did not like, which basically involved anything that had to do with leaving the office. Life was good.

Then, in the late 1980s and early 1990s the landscape of the industry changed, and clients started to leave us. Our fees were not the cheapest around, and, in an effort to curb expenses, clients searched for and found cheaper alternatives. By remaining nameless and faceless, I had inadvertently commoditized my business.

Those who stayed had developed a relationship with me. Furthermore, these clients, on top of being loyal, were, by and large, the most profitable clients that I had. They were also the most prolific in referring new clients to our firm. So the first thing I decided that I needed to do was to begin to bring in business. I had never done this before and was not really sure where to begin or if I would be any good at it. I was reasonably confident that I could do it, but I just was not exactly sure how to go about it.

An insurance agent, whom I had become friendly with, had joined an organization known as the Metropolitan Business Network. He was enthusiastic about the people and the results (new business leads and referrals) that it was producing for him. I wanted to see if this might be something that could work for me. My insurance friend initially discouraged me from coming down and evaluating it. He said that what my firm did was so esoteric that my opportunities to acquire new business would be limited. He also said that if retirement plans ever came up for discussion, he would make sure that it was directed to me anyway.

Buried under my actuarial skin lives a competitive human being. Tell me that I cannot accomplish something and I will set out to prove you wrong. Furthermore, I did not want someone else deciding what might or might not be an appropriate business opportunity for my firm.

In my initial MBN meeting, I stood in front of about fifty people and explained what my firm did. I then answered a few questions from the members. It has been said that public speaking ranks second on the food chain of what people fear most (the first may involve being locked in a room with an actuary; I am not entirely sure). Shy though I may be, for some reason, public speaking is something that does not daunt me.

The first meeting went very well, as did the second. I was offered a membership and gladly accepted. At one of the early meetings, the member who occupied the financial brokerage slot told me that she knew that one of her clients was somewhat unhappy with the firm handling their company's pension plan. She suggested that I call and meet with the president.

What goes through your mind when you are given a referral like this? Doubt, a lot of doubt. Does this person really want to talk to me? Aren't I bothering them? Are they going to be dismissive? Are they going to confuse me with someone (horrors!) selling life insurance? All those thoughts, and a few more, floated through my head. I made the call anyway. The president of this firm (which employed about three hundred people) could not have been nicer. He was very unhappy with his current relationship but was not ready to take any action at that time. He asked me to call him in about three months. I interpreted his response as a nice way of blowing me off.

I did call in three months (probably on the twenty-fourth hour of the third month). I pictured what would happen when I followed up. He would not remember me, or he would remember me but not take the call. If he took the call, he would tell me that they were still not ready to do anything. That would be followed by something like, "Why don't you call again in three or four months?"

Imagine my shock when he asked me to send a written proposal about the services we would provide along with the fees. The engagement letter went out the next day and was signed and returned by overnight mail the day after he received it. I had worked harder on bringing in plans with one or two people than this client who maintained two pension plans for his three-hundred-odd employees.

I guess there was something to this networking thing after all. I learned some lessons. One, don't always listen to that little voice in your head. Don't dismiss it, but don't necessarily let it rule your life either. What is the worst thing that can happen if I act on this? In my example, the president of this company may have been dismissive. So what? Would any real damage have been done? Did I stand to gain more than I could lose?

I passed leads on to others in the group when I could (when I was comfortable doing so). I joined the board, and this honor helped make me feel like I had become something of an accomplished networker.

One of the things that keep the MBN fresh and is absolutely essential to its ongoing well-being is its guests. Guests can turn into potential members, and, even if they do not, very often a connection is made between the guest and a current member. Relationships are forged, opportunities are identified, and business is very often exchanged.

I rarely brought guests. Jeff Meshel, however, was prolific in producing guests. Why was that? Well, Jeff was very enthusiastic about the MBN and extolled its virtues to almost everyone he met. I was just the opposite. I rarely discussed it with my clients because it did not seem to be an appropriate topic.

At that time, my meetings with my clients were entirely focused on my firm and what I could do for them. This was not done out of arrogance. It was precipitated more out of a lack of confidence. I rarely asked them what sort of business they were in, nor did I inquire as to what sort of help they might be looking for. I worked very hard to get business referrals, and they rarely (and this is significant) came from my clients. One day, I asked Jeffrey for help. We started to review my client list. "What does this company do?" he asked. I did not know.

Jeffrey felt quite strongly that many companies viewed what I did as a commodity. People could get their retirement plan done by almost anyone. Yes, perhaps we were smarter and paid more attention to detail. However, would that be enough to attract the size and type of clients that I wanted? Even the process of entertaining such a thought was painful. How many times had I lost out to an inferior firm simply because of price? More than I would care to admit. This was especially true if the client had no real sense of who we were. In other words, if a third party (an accountant, a financial planner, etc.) had referred them, they really had no connection at all to our firm. Clearly, if I had the problem, so did other professionals—attorneys, accountants, and so on.

So Jeffrey and I began to explore what would begin to change us from a commodity to a resource to our clients. And then Jeffrey had a second insight. He said we were in the wrong business. It was the assets within our client's retirement plans, not the consulting aspect, that represented the true opportunity. Here is where I needed to draw the line. Clearly, Jeffrey was wrong. He did not know what he was talking about. What did I know about investments? I would have to get licensed, and the sum total of my investment expertise was that I read *The Wall Street Journal*.

And yet, on both counts, Jeffrey was dead on. We had become a commodity to most of our clients. And how many times had we designed and installed a 401(k) plan where the client had requested help in placing the assets with the appropriate financial institution?

I began to meet with my clients to explore with them certain questions: What did they do? How was business? What did they need help with? How could I help? (And if I couldn't, would I know where to go?)

I never promised to help everyone that I met, nor do people really expect that. However, if you listen carefully and try to help people, most are extremely grateful for the effort (whether you are successful or not) and remember it. People start to view you as a resource that extends far beyond your core business. And when that shift takes place, you are no longer a commodity but a value-added entity. So I began to ask questions and keep notes (one of Jeffrey's mantras). Once I understood what my clients did, it became easier to match their needs with certain services or products that other people I knew could provide.

I also decided to address the issue of the investment side of my business. I acquired the appropriate licenses. After doing due diligence, I formed an alliance with certain insurance companies that had entered the 401(k) business. They provided the links with various mutual funds and allowed employees daily access via an 800 number or the Internet. We were able to link our computers with theirs so that when participants made a change in their investment allocation, or had a question on their account, we could see it and respond to it. Because we were providing services that the insurance company no longer needed to staff up for, on top of our usual fees, the insurance company paid us an override out of the plan assets. With this alliance and the talents we already had (consulting, plan design, superior service), we began to rebuild our firm.

Although it pains me to admit it, Jeffrey was right. I was in the wrong business. Would I have come to this conclusion on my own? Probably. Would it have happened with the alacrity that it did without Jeffrey pushing me? Probably not.

Of course, I began introducing some of my clients and contacts to Jeffrey. One of his core businesses is providing bridge loans. One of the first clients I had introduced Jeffrey to was the president of a large manufacturing firm in New York City. He and Jeffrey hit it off and became quite close and as a result my client and I became closer.

Networking is a two-way street. If all you do is get and you do not strive to give, the fruits will be short-lived. This raises the question of what have I done for others. Help provided to other people is not always business that you refer to them. A doctor client of mine called me a few months ago and asked for my help. He said that his son had decided on a career as an attorney. Could I help find him a summer position as an unpaid intern? Right now, with the economy being what it is, many law firms are not as flush as they used to be. Law school students are happy to get unpaid internships. Given that fact, why would a law firm bring on board a college student? I told my client that, as a result of networking, I knew many partners in law firms, both large and small. I also told him the reality of the situation, and I told him I would do my best.

The answer that I got from everyone I called was pretty much what I expected: We have cut back on our own staff, we are not hiring for the summer, etc. But a partner that I met through the Strategic Forum surprised me. He told me that, yes, he or one of his partners could use some help for the summer (database entry, that sort of thing). He would make some inquiries and give my client's son a call. An unpaid position actually materialized out of that phone call. Now, what do you think my client will remember? The professional and unique job we did designing and maintaining his retirement plan or the fact that through networking his son was able to secure a summer position?

Now, I did not enjoy making those phone calls for help. In fact, I found the whole process extremely distasteful. I felt that I was being intrusive and requesting a favor from people whom I did not know all that well. It is important to know that those are *my* feelings. The partners that I spoke to at the various law firms could not have been nicer, even the ones that could not help. With all of my hesitation and concern that I was being perceived as a nuisance, a result was produced and a client relationship was cemented.

Anyone can make networking work for them. You may not feel comfortable doing it. You may think that you are too shy or withdrawn. You would be making a mistake. It is not really important how you feel when you ask for help. The important thing is to find a way to do it that works for you, a way that reflects who you are as a person. And I can tell you, when someone calls and thanks you for going a little out of your way, *there is no money in the world that can replicate that feeling.*

You may need to start at the shallow end of the pool. But take the plunge. Your business and personal life may change in ways that you could never have imagined.

15

The Rewards of Networking

As I've mentioned throughout the book, the one driving motivation I have for being the hub of a large network is the great feeling I get from helping others. In the previous chapter, David Gensler said there was no amount of money that could compensate for this feeling. This is a fundamental tenet that you should not forget. You cannot move forward if you're constantly thinking, *"What will he do for me?"* or *"Now, he owes me a favor."* This is not about the "favor bank." It's not about Seinfeld's comment "He owes me large." Networking can only work well if you do it with no expectations other than it will make you better at what you do, and generally better at doing business.

There are two kinds of resisters to my philosophy. The first type is the one who is dogmatic and disagreeable. They think they're as good as they can be, and no advice or criticism from me or anyone else will ever convince them otherwise. I don't waste any time or effort in trying to change someone who doesn't think they need to change.

The second type of resister is more of a mystery. I'm often frustrated when I see people who do need help in expanding their network, and, while they are quick to admit their shortcomings, they fail to do anything about it. I take these failures far too personally because not everyone who wants help is a candidate for change. They just *think* they want help but are either afraid or unwilling to do something about it. As a committed facilitator and persuader, this type of person perplexes me but also continues to energize me. I don't give up easily, and neither should you.

Conversely, I do often take pleasure when people are agreeable to my advice. Doug Garr, who was my collaborator on this book, is one modest example of a networking-improvement project. At one point, Garr attended a book publishing party where

 Rule 34 Get out more often. The view of the world from behind your desk is a narrow one.

he thought about some of my concepts and put them to work immediately. He recalled, "I came prepared. I stuck a bunch of business cards in my suit coat pocket so I could reach for one and still hold a cocktail in the other hand. Simple, but I almost laughed when I saw everyone around me fumbling for his or her business cards.

"I started out a little bit on the shy side, saying hello to the four or five people I knew at the event. I thought this was a natural way of warming up, however, and as people excused themselves to get a drink or an hors d'oeuvre, I forced myself to get up the courage to break into conversations with people I didn't know.

"I just went up and introduced myself to three people talking and asked them their connection to the author and what they did. I listened for a few minutes, and they eventually asked me why I was there and what I did. One guy immediately asked me for my card, saying he thought it was fascinating that I was a speechwriter for CEOs of large companies. He wanted to get into that as well, and I said, 'Just let me know what I can do. I'd be glad to help you.' Later, he called me, and we talked for some time on the phone about the process and how to break in. Probably nothing will happen from it, but that's not the point, is it? And at least it was a start.

"With another group, I repeated the names of five people when we were introduced, and I made it a point to use their names when we were talking, and I remembered the names of all five people. This was unusual for me because I'm basically lousy at names."

He left the publishing party with six new business contacts, and he put their names immediately in his e-mail address book with the appropriate annotations. Garr is obviously on his way to getting it. He understands the value of mixing it up, expanding his network, and using some of the precepts of this book.

The good thing about networking is that it almost always requires you to stray from behind your desk. It's easier to network in an airport lounge where you don't know anyone than it is over a tense, formal business lunch where you're meeting somebody for the first time. People are more approachable, their defenses are lowered, it's easier to evolve toward a conversation. This is why the golf course is such a popular place to network and build relationships. You're spending four or five hours with a few other people playing a gentleman's game with long-standing customs, where a certain amount of camaraderie is unleashed. It's a seductive environment. You need not take up golf to become a good networker, but you should get out of your office on a regular basis.

Learn how to waste time creatively. Be bold, even when you risk being criticized for bad behavior. In a recent story on networking in *The New York Times,* a conversation on a plane began when a man eavesdropped on his seatmate's work and made a comment about it. The woman sitting next to him said, "I thought, '*How dare he look over my shoulder like that?*' But we started chatting." Five years later, the two are still referring business to each other.

Be bold. Years ago at the Byron Nelson tournament in Irving, Texas, golf legend Tom Kite and Dr. Bob Rotella, a sports psychologist, were having lunch with a teaching pro from Texas who had two young students who qualified for the event. The pro said his guys were really nervous because they hadn't played with anyone really good. Kite said what they should do is walk up to the best guys on tour and say, "I'd love to play a practice round with you." But they would have to begin by having the nerve to ask. Similarly, you shouldn't be afraid to seek advice from the luminaries in your industry and ask them out to lunch or dinner. More often than not, they'll be flattered someone called. Listen and get ideas about how to succeed.

Rule 35 — Stay balanced—contentment is success.

Isiah Thomas, the great Detroit Pistons basketball player, recalled that when he was a rookie in 1982, he decided to seek out Kareem Abdul-Jabbar at the All-Star game. He wanted some advice about how to go about winning in the NBA. At the time Abdul-Jabbar had a reputation for being aloof and unapproachable. Thomas was invited to meet with Abdul-Jabbar. "He was very kind and gracious," Thomas said. "He gave me about two hours in his room, just talking."

Was this the beginning of a business networking conversation? You be the judge. In the spring of 2004, Thomas, now the New York Knicks president, hired Abdul-Jabbar as a West Coast scout for his team. Sometimes relationships take a long time to nurture and grow, and the results of your efforts aren't apparent until much later.

There's a limit, of course, to how much time you want to devote to networking. It is real work, after all, and it is time consuming. And too many people, as hard as they try, cannot get over certain levels of discomfort. Think about Gensler when he is asked for a favor, and he has to make phone calls trying to place a student in a summer job during a difficult economy. In the end, however, most people welcomed his so-called intrusion.

So I urge you to make that phone call, especially when you dread having to do it. Don't worry about the results. Good things will happen when you least expect it. Set aside a certain amount of time each day—say an hour—when you'll do nothing but sift through your database and make phone calls and renew old contacts. Force yourself to do this no matter how busy you are. You'll be surprised when connections and reconnections begin to pan out. Again, remember, you're doing this because you want to help your friends and colleagues first.

Finally, remember that while you can measure your networking success in tangible results, this should not be your ultimate goal. Success, as we all know, is defined in many different ways.

Appendix

Join Paradigm V, the Ultimate Networking Experiment

Welcome to Paradigm V. The ultimate networking resource! Become a member of Paradigm V and instantly connect with experts and professionals around the world. Paradigm V will let you quickly access their business interests, skill sets, board affiliations, passions, and ultimately allow you to find the information, expertise, and connections *you* need!

Paradigm V is the ultimate resource for enhancing every business opportunity that comes your way.

HOW DOES IT WORK?

To join, you will need to create a username and password. Once registered, you'll fill out a template like the one I have filled out below. Let's use mine as an example.

WHAT YOU NEED TO KNOW ABOUT ME

Mercury Capital Inc.
Jeffrey Meshel
President
380 Lexington Ave
Suite 2020
New York, N.Y. 10168

(T) 212-661-8700 x229
(F) 212-661-8831
Email: jeffm@mercurycap.com
Industry: Real Estate/Investments

Business Interests

A) Real Estate Bridge Loans: Mercury Capital funds them as a Principal
B) <u>Real Estate Acquisitions:</u> Mercury Properties buys commercial, residential, and industrial real estate
C) Raise Capital:
    1) For both Public and Private Companies
    2) <u>Municipal Bond</u> and <u>Cash Management</u> Assets
    3) <u>Real Estate Bridge Loans</u>
    4) <u>Hedge Funds</u>
    5) <u>P.I.P.E.S.</u>
    6) <u>S.P.A.C.s</u>

Skill Sets

<u>Networking</u>, Real Estate Expertise, Lending Expertise, <u>Investments</u>

Passions

Physical Fitness, <u>Wine</u>

Board Affiliations

1. <u>The Strategic Forum</u> (Chairman)
    a) An organization of business leaders from diverse backgrounds dedicated to the exchange of ideas, development of long-term personal and business relationships, and the facilitation of business opportunities among members and their respective networks
2. <u>Broadband Capital</u> (Advisory Board)
    a) Boutique Investment Bank focusing on <u>China</u>, <u>Reverse Mergers</u>, S.P.A.C.s, and <u>Public/Private Equity</u>

What I Need!

1. Real estate lending opportunities that a conventional lender can't do
2. Introductions to Hedge Funds that make investments in micro-cap companies, S.P.A.C. Transactions, P.I.P.E.S., and Private Equity
3. Introductions to Municipal Bond investors, including SWAPS and Cash Management
4. Introductions to Entrepreneurs in transition who are looking for something to do

Once you have completed the form, you're ready to create your key words or search indices like those I have underlined above. These key words will also enable other members to search for and find you, your information, and needs in the Paradigm V database!

With your profile complete, you are now ready to connect with other members in the database.

A PICTURE IS WORTH A THOUSAND WORDS!

Imagine you've just entered the cosmetics business and plan to sell your product via infomercials. You're under way but missing some key parts; i.e., the right packaging, proper funding, etc.

Imagine Paradigm V having 1,000,000 members whose expertise and connections are now available to you at the push of a button. You will be able to instantly view all of the Paradigm V key words listed in alphabetical order, locate the ones you need—like cosmetics expert, infomercial expert, packaging expert, branding expert—and then submit your query.

The Paradigm V system will instantly search the database and report back to you that, for example, 1,172 members have these key words in their profile. Then the system will respond, "Tell us more about what you need," and you will be able to explain your requirements in greater detail in the space provided. Then once completed, your detailed request will be e-mailed to those 1,172 members. Those interested in connecting with you will respond so you can take the next step in building your business. And theirs!

What a time saver! What a networking opportunity! What a way to give yourself and your business an edge!

Paradigm V. Go to our Web site now and join www.paradigmv. com.

Index